WHOLE-ASS

WHOLE-ASS

Stop living a half-assed life and
enjoy an extraordinary existence.

So you can play your part in
making this world a better place.

MAHARANI

To all sorts of asses out there...

This edition is published by
That Guy's House in 2019

www.ThatGuysHouse.com

Hey,

Welcome to this wonderful book brought to you by That Guy's House Publishing.

At That Guy's House we believe in real and raw wellness books that inspire the reader from a place of authenticity and honesty.

This book has been carefully crafted by both the author and publisher so that it will bring you hope, inspiration and sensation of inner peace.

It is our hope that you thoroughly enjoy this book and pass it onto somebody who may also be in need of a glimpse into their own magnificence.

Have a wonderful day.

Love,

Sean Patrick

That Guy.

www.ThatGuysHouse.com

Contents

Foreword

The concepts of human growth, personal development, and mental health can be challenging to understand. For many of us, new learnings go against the way we have thought and lived for much of our lives. Our mind - desperate to keep us safe - would rather have us remain in our comfort zone, staying as we already are.

It takes something special to push our boundaries, something that talks to us in a unique way that encourages us to see a new, fresh perspective that invites us to see things differently. Right from the beginning, this book did exactly that, prodding my insecurities and having me question my comfort zones, it talked to me in a way I haven't experienced before. Sometimes uncomfortably, always impactfully.

In a world that encourages us to conform rather than flourish, this comes from a refreshingly accessible and relatable place. If you're looking to grow in any form, it's going to talk to you on some level, showing you the paths that perhaps you have found yourself taking without intention.

It will specifically question your intention and determination to step away from half-hearted (or half-assed as I'd now say) living that is much the easier and safer choice. Half-assed fits in with society's expectations that provides us with pats on our backs, it impresses others but doesn't impress our own truth. It looks ok on the outside but it feels half empty and often comes at a cost: our own hopes and dreams. This book will invite you to swap ticking boxes for a life that feels purposeful and meaningful, a life that makes you deeply proud of who we are.

I believe the universe is constantly providing us with reminders. As I read this book, I learned that a friend of a friend lost her life to a traffic road accident in central London. Young, talented and living a purposeful existence, she had so much going for her. As I heard the horrific news, I returned to the book to be reminded further quite how precious life is, do we really want to live it half-heartedly, with a knowing within that we didn't give our all?

Sometimes it's difficult to establish where our soul most craves growth, this book will provide you with the pokes and probs to jump into the unknown, the space where whole-ass living exists.

Having been on a similar journey to the author in many ways myself, there are points within the book that nerves are touched, I've become reawakened to the fact that I'm still a little raw in some areas. I'm grateful for the reminder that none of us will get to a point in our lives where we have all the answers, we must continue to challenge ourselves because without growth there will always be some kind of connection to emptiness.

As I progressed through these pages I found a reawakening within me in areas where I thought I had moved on. It's amazing how different language and ways of thinking can reinvigorate an energy within, it's given me the kick up the ass to keep living purposefully, push boundaries and to actively seek growth again internally.

Ben Bidwell,

The Naked Professor

Preface

Why are people wasting their lives away? Why do they commit to one thing or another, do that thing in diluted mode, and then blame the thing for not providing fulfillment? It's senseless, unproductive and, honestly, to me, just a waste of time.

I am a monk. I have a spiritual teacher. I have committed to a path of Oneness. I've taken vows. I have a lot of monk colleagues, and yet, a few years ago, when I started developing a close relationship with one of the monks, I noticed that his approach to the path was different to mine. He was hardly even on the path, doing the bare minimum and being committed only when it was convenient. Even though he loved the teaching, there was no real vibration and going-for-it-ness. As a result, his path was harder and he wasn't having such a good time.

In an attempt to try to explain to him that his half-assed approach was the root of him not enjoying the path fully, I started writing a booklet. First, I sent it to him, and then I sent it out to all of my fellow monks with a desire to inspire them. It was called: "Be Whole-Ass: How to stop half-assing your way to freedom."

It was concise, short and intended only for our group, but then a desire to share this information with anyone that wants to stop messing around and actually have fun in life started growing, and the will to write a book was alive in me. However, I needed help giving some structure to my ideas, as a booklet or a blog is definitely not the same as a book!

It was not so long after when, at a retreat, we had an auction to raise money for a documentary about our teaching. One of the other teachers had written 11 books, and he offered to put up for auction a coaching package on how to write a book. Even though I thought I didn't need it, when the time came, my arm kept lifting and I kept bidding until I won the item. It's so strange when one of your limbs moves on it's own!

Next thing I knew, I was on a mountain in Coletta, northern Italy, giving shape to this project, starting a relationship with the writer dude and falling in love with Limoncello.

Fifteen months later, here I am.

Acknowledgements

Sutratman, my heart goes out in gratefulness to you. None of these words would've been possible without your guidance, your time, and your accurate questions. The way you believe in me and what I have to say to the world inspires me to be the best version of myself every day. Thank you for always raising the bar as a partner, a writer and a human being. I love you so much, and it is such a pleasure to walk with you, my incredible fiancé.

Maharishi Krishnananda, your teaching is present in every cell in my body and in every word I write. You are my Teacher, my friend, my relationship counselor, my manager, my whip and the guy who shows me the newest trends in songs and videos. Thank you for reminding me of the Truth and what really matters. Thank you for saving my vision of humanity and helping me see that underneath it all, there is only love.

To my mother, wherever you are, spread in the stars and watching over me. Thank you for living full on until the last living breath you had. Thank you for letting me fly and letting me discover my path. I feel your love every single day, and my only hope is that you are as proud of me as I am of how you led your life.

To my dad, Daniel, you are the most amazing man. Thank you for being the constant whole-ass, joyful kid you are. Your love for service, your talent and your desire to build a better world through education goes with me wherever I go. I am so blessed to be your daughter and to have inherited your genes. There is no stop in you, and you taught me to always follow my truth and my dreams.

To Maitreya, because you were the first person to ever read this book. You pushed me to keep going, and you always make me laugh, out loud, until my belly hurts.

To Ishani, for being the best of friends and a constant source of support. No distance is real when I have you on the other side of my phone, always accepting me as I am and reminding me what I am capable of. We started this journey together, and my words and your images are always intertwined. You are my type of weird – my soulmate of jokes, talks and intensity balls.

To Rama, Satta, Dharma Raj, Jaya, Manyu, Narain, Dayavati, Saraswati and Maharati, Alexia and Sandunga. Our conversations spark my creativity, and by letting myself unravel like an old sweater I found my way on these pages. There is nothing bigger than friendship. You guys rock my world.

To every single member of my family. I am lucky to belong to the coolest, craziest, whole-assed family. Every single one of you is a huge statement of living, giving, loving and dropping the mic, every single day. Especially to Mar, for having a better vision of the design than I could ever come up with and for going all-in with me.

And a huge, huge thanks to Sean and That Guy's House for believing in me, in this project and in the message I have. Thanks to Mathew McKeown for turning my version of English into proper English and to Peter Watkins for his patience and help in putting this book together.

Introduction:

WHOLE-ASS

What's in it for you?

To be whole-ass, you need to get rid of all those attitudes that stop you from engaging with life with an open heart and an open self.

Why would you want to do that? Well, if you want a life of freedom and greatness that is worth living, fully enjoying every single relationship you have, then living whole-ass is the way to go.

Being you, the Real You, giving absolutely everything you've got while going beyond any perceived limitations, defenses, fear, hesitation or doubts is the only way to fully engage every single moment you live. And whole-assing the moment leads to whole-assing your life.

Discovery, growth, joy, a sense of connection, experiencing love and feeling life coursing through your veins are all habits that you can develop to create a fantastic way of being that will not only propel your life into extraordinariness, but will also impact and inspire others around you to do the same.

It is not for everyone, of course. Many people will still prefer mediocrity, because living fully requires getting off the couch and shedding multiple skins until you become bigger and brighter than before.

But it's my sense, or maybe my desire, that most humans crave a life of plenitude, bliss and peace; to wake up with a huge smile on their face and then carry it right through the day, talking through a grin to all their loved ones, before going to bed sore from all that smiling.

In this book, I will attempt to sum up the attitudes and habits needed to shake the half-assness from your life and rock the most important relationship you will ever know: the one you have with yourself.

From there, every other relationship, every encounter and every activity you do will certainly be lived with nothing left in the account for a rainy day. Everything comes into our life for a reason, and the way to discover these reasons is to be full on, whole-ass.

Whole-assed. Wholehearted. Whole.

PART 1

"People pretend not to like
grapes when the vines are too
high for them to reach."

Marguerite de Navarre

Chapter 1

Sleep, Repeat, Die

My dad used to call me Runaway Bride. I do not look like Julia Roberts, although I do have a big mouth, nor do I wear dresses with running shoes. Actually, who am I kidding? Sometimes I do. He called me that because running away was the thing I did best.

You don't believe me? Let's do some math:

College years:

Studied at 7 different universities...

... in 3 different countries

... in 5 different cities

... in 11 different apartments

... tried 12 different degrees.

... finished none.

I am not even going to do the math on relationships. Let's not even go there. Let's not count. I'll just repeat the term: "Runaway Bride." There is a reason behind it.

I've had serious relationships, not-so-serious relationships and sex friends. I've been engaged and had a marriage that later turned into a relationship. I've dated guys from seven different countries. I've lived with boyfriends and been in both monogamous relationships and not-so-monogamous ones. I've played a housewife, I've been a muse and I've dumped and been dumped.

I've loved someone who didn't love me back and I've had to break the heart of someone I didn't love. I've longed for years for the one that got away, and I've been the object of desire of the one I ran away from. I've been in love with my best friend and I've cheated and been cheated on. I've doubted my sexual orientation, only to run back to it 30 minutes later.

I've moved countries chasing an ideal that ended in tears, and I've moved cities and discovered that being intrepid is actually a good thing. I've been single for years and then a serial monogamist just as long. I've believed in fairy tales, and I have also believed that this whole thing called life is nothing other than a cosmic joke.

I do not know if I have tried it all, but I am pretty sure I've tried a lot.

Throughout my 20s, I thought I was living life fully, to the maximum. The world seemed like a buffet to me, and I was constantly hungry. I was so proud of myself for being full on.

Was I happy?

No.

Was I living fully?

I've since discovered that no, I wasn't.

Always striving for the perfect life – one without a single dull moment – I had fallen into the scariest trap of them all: half-ass.

My hungry guts were constantly empty. Nothing was digesting, nothing was nourishing enough and nothing was giving me satisfaction. No pleasure, challenge or novelty could last, and even if it did, I was constantly asking myself if there was something better around the corner.

I felt like a Viking, constantly sinking my teeth into a big piece of meat, only to spit it out after sucking out all the flavor.

Life was at my feet and I was living everything half-full. I knew I could do anything I wanted, I was built that way, and yet I wasn't fulfilled.

I was missing the point of being alive.

A PERSPECTIVE FROM A HALF-ASS VIEW

You probably remember a time, a long, long time ago, when you attended kindergarten, and life seemed to be incredibly fluid and joyful.

Now, however, the world seems to be full of angry or annoying people, and you guess that the wonderful experience you once had was only meant for little kids. Adults do not get to have that. OK, maybe some do, but it's probably due to the alignment of their planets, or else they are just really lucky people born in a golden crib.

You have a job and some activities going on in your life. You pay your bills and probably own a house, or at least you'd like to. You are doing everything you are supposed to. Heck, you even go on vacations with the family! However, peace and happiness remain fleeting experiences that you constantly feel the need to keep grasping at or topping up.

You probably have a relationship or marriage that is good, but not great, filled with complications and awkward silences. You wish it could be easier, you wish you could be seen, and you sometimes wonder if this is all there is. But hey, it's better than nothing, and you are too old or too involved to change it now.

Perhaps you are single, trying on relationships like shirts at a mall, or avoiding them as if they were the devil incarnate. Maybe amazing relationships based on growth, giving, constant joy and flow only happen to a few chosen ones, because those people were blessed by cupid's kiss.

You have friends, but you long for those days when you were younger and conversations went deeper. That time when you could actually hang out and have quality time together, when friends were a big part of your life. Now you are lucky if you see them once a month.

You wonder if this is the life you are meant to live.

If you encounter a big challenge, and if it happens to match your schedule, you start some sort of regime to make your life better, and you feel happy for a while. You even start to consider the possibility that the world can be a happy place, and happiness and contentment seem within reach. Eventually, that feeling fades, and life seems stagnant again. You didn't get it, and you quickly get used to that.

Maybe a few fleeting moments of aliveness is all you will get in this lifetime?

ONCE UPON A TIME...

Once upon a time, there was a little boy who wanted to do so many things in life. He imagined that when he grew up, he would be huge. He had this sense that he had been put on Earth to do something really purposeful and important, and that he'd probably be a famous artist or a Nobel Prize winner.

He thought he could have it all.

Then, he grew up.

He gave it a shot or two, thinking that life would roll out the red carpet for him once the world knew of his existence. But life seemed to have a life of its own, and there were actual challenges to meet! His dreams of greatness weren't immediately realized when and how he wanted.

And he wept.

A great life obviously wasn't for him, and he would have to settle. Oh, he was such a victim of this mean, terrible life! He might as well give up and leave the big dreams to other, luckier people. He probably didn't have a purpose for breathing, except to just get through the days.

Wake up.

Have a coffee.

Drag his feet around.

Go to work.

Worry about bills.

Dream of vacations.

Get drunk after work.

Say the things he doesn't dare to when sober.

Sleep.

Repeat.

Forever.

When the little boy became a teenager, he fell in love, and then he got his heart broken by a teenage girl. A human being falling in love and then experiencing heartbreak? How bizarre!

And he shut down.

It set him off on a series of failed relationships that never seemed quite right. It was probably all the women he met. They were all unsuitable for him. He was doomed, the poor little boy.

One time, he even dated a girl whose music taste was completely different to his. How daring! How intrepid! Of course, he eventually broke it off, since this was not the basis of a healthy, successful relationship.

He had a rule: "Once I know I'm with the girl of my dreams; once I know she is the woman I am going to marry, then, and only then, will I give it my all."

Before he knew it, the little boy was not so little anymore. He was a grown-ass man, still living in his parents games room, still daydreaming about leaving his hometown, and still imagining that one day life will magically change, and he will wake up living the life of his dreams, in his house on the beach, creating away.

Don't get me wrong, he kinda liked his job. He kinda liked his city. He kinda liked his income and he kinda liked his friends.

He kinda liked himself.

Grown man fell in love again. It happened against all odds, because life does surprise you sometimes, even when you have closed all doors. He promised many things that one day he would do with this girl. He promised to give her a bouquet of gardenias and sing her a song. He had quite a lovely voice, but he rarely sang, because it was never quite the right moment. Above all else, he promised to love her.

But then he backtracked, remembering his rule.

Months passed, and he never gave or did any of the things he promised. It still wasn't safe to know if she was the one, so why would he ever do these things? It wouldn't make sense!

And one day, he was alone again.

And he kept wondering why life wasn't full, or anything like what he expected. Why couldn't life just cut-him-a break? Why didn't things change?

He was indeed a lovely guy. Everyone liked him. He was kind, funny, loving and smart.

Sleep.

Repeat.

For years.

And then he died.

"The quickest way to kill the human spirit
is to ask someone to do mediocre work."

Ayn Rand

MEDIOCRITY IS THE NOT-SO-NEW PLAGUE

Ordinariness. Flatline. Minimum effort. Average. Common places. Passing through. Being invisible.

You go to the coffee house and the clerk is not quite there. She is checking her phone with one hand and taking your order with the other.

You call your phone company, and you are not sure if you are talking to a robot or an actual person. Whatever you say, you get the same freaking scripted response.

You get a new idea and ask someone at work if something can be done. "Oh, I don't know, it's really complicated," they say, and then go back to their screen.

You wonder if people are actually inside their bodies. 'Hello!!! Is anyone in there?' You eventually get so frustrated that you decide to do the same. Just finish this day. Just pass through.

No one seems to be quite enjoying what they are doing. How would life be if everyone, from the cleaning clerk to the director of the UN, was actually enjoying, with complete enthusiasm, whatever they were doing?

Mediocrity is not new. Its original definition was "halfway up a mountain." Get excited about something, start it, arrive halfway, get comfortable, eat a 7-Eleven sandwich and forget about getting to the top. After all, you probably didn't really want to get any higher in the first place.

Mediocrity means staying in the middle, neither here nor there.

Have you ever been on a sidewalk and there is someone walking in front of you, slowly, right in the middle, so that you cannot pass them on the left or right? They are oblivious to the fact that their middle walking is affecting other people's journeys to their destinations. Everything behind them starts stagnating, with people cramping up behind.

Everybody sighs in relief once that person decides to move over and stare at a window or something. Order is restored.

Mediocrity is not to be confused with neutrality. I am talking about an extended belief in humankind, which says that we take for granted the fact that we are a walking miracle, made of stardust, with an elastic machine that allows us to experience life through the senses; to feel love and to see the colors and benevolence of this planet called Earth.

A belief that as humans, we somehow came to simply use up oxygen, pay bills, be kind of happy and then die.

Each one of us is a miracle. I am not saying anything new, but can you see it? You were inside someone's belly once, the product of a moment where an ovule and a sperm decided to love each other and create life. That is no accident. You are no accident.

You are a freaking walking miracle.

The story of the sad little boy is based on a true story, let's call him Gardenia Guy. I got to see front row how an amazing human being full of potential, full of life, with the natural ability to live the life he wanted and to impact others, can remain small due to a belief that he is not worth it.

Such a shame. It's not only a waste of someone's life, but also of the possibility to make this world a better place by impacting other people's lives. A human being not living life in utter joy, feeling in every moment that they are living their purpose, is so discombobulating to me.

We all have a purpose. We all have it in us.
We need to discover what that is.

It's always fed my fire to help people to reach out for more. From whatever platform I've been standing on since I was a stubborn little girl, it's always sparked my fire to spark other people's fires.

Then again, as a good friend told me the other day, I don't have to want to marry everyone I want to help, because there are millions out there. "Imagine the lifetimes it would take you," he said.

And that's when I learned not to half-ass my path to walk someone else's, and to stop waiting for a sad little boy to give me any gardenias.

"Never half-ass two things.
Whole-ass one thing."

Ron Swanson,
(Parks and Recreation, 2012)

Chapter 2

The Habits of Highly Half-Assed People

Have you ever had to share a seat with someone, with half your ass hanging off the edge? It takes acrobatic abilities to maintain your cool. It's effortful, distracting and off-balancing. That's why I love the term 'half-ass'. It is so pure. So descriptive.

Would you believe me if I told you that our natural state is to live every moment effortlessly engaged in what is happening in front of us, completely present and not being distracted by the constant stream of thought that pull us out of the moment?

> *Whole-assing every moment*
> *leads to a whole-ass life.*

Remember a time when you fell in love, or when you really liked someone. Got it? Now, remember one of the first encounters, probably having dinner or hanging out on the couch at your parent's house, wishing that your mom extended your curfew for at least a half-hour.

Were you distracted by the noise in the restaurant? No. Were you concerned about school the next day? No. Were you thinking about the political situation in Rwanda? No. You were fully there, delighted with the amazing human being in front of you and completely engaged with what was happening. If anything, you would get a bit distracted by a feeling of "how did I ever get so lucky?"

It may seem that the state of fullness you experienced in that moment was a product of having the object of your affection, but what if it was the other way around? What if the reason behind experiencing such awe is because you were completely and effortlessly attentive in the present moment?

Maybe in the previous case, your attention was so present because the object in front of you created such fascination. But in the same way that sometimes we don't fall in love with someone until we fully *see* them, chances are we don't fully see what is in front of us unless we are properly attentive. With that level of attention, most things will probably provoke a sense of awe.

I used to be an actress, and absolutely adored the rush of being in a play. I disappeared into the moment, and magic happened on stage. Life was full, exciting and alive, happening right there and then. I was constantly being put in a place where I had to be open, raw and vulnerable.

I was whole-ass about it. With all my heart, body and soul I'd engage that activity. The rest of my activities and endeavors weren't like that, but it planted the seed. If I can live one part of my life wholehearted, can I live the rest of it that way?

It's the nature of your heart to be whole-ass.
The heart aches when it is not living fully.

But now, let's cut to the chase...

ARE YOU HALF-ASS?

I don't think anyone wants to brag about being half-ass. We probably hide it even from ourselves, justifying our half-ass existence with 1,000 different excuses.

However, I promise you, I won't tell. If you are willing to look at yourself in all honesty and discover your level of half-assness, I won't tell a soul.

Be honest, you already know the answer. The areas where you have been half-assing your existence are being smashed in your face constantly. It takes one moment of brutal honesty, one moment of stopping all those excuses you give yourself, and a willingness to not take any of them seriously any longer.

First step: Own it. If you are a half-ass, own it.

Imagine you are walking around with one eye open and one eye closed. That's how you walk – or drive – to work, that's how you talk to your best friend over coffee and that's how you watch a film in the movie theater.

It's a funny image that one, humans going about their lives with only one eye open. Try it for half an hour. You'll notice that not only do you look ridiculous, but also that you miss out on many things, and that it is so effortful it will probably make you dizzy.

That's the perfect metaphor for being half-ass.

You are half awake and half asleep.

Have you ever tried to have a conversation super early in the morning, after a difficult night when you woke up knackered and groggy? I'll tell you what happens for me: I do not make sense, I don't give clear answers, I don't understand correctly what is happening and I don't even know what the other person is saying. For Christ's sake, I am asleep. Leave me alone!

My mom used to hate that. Before she went to work, she would ask me to run some errands, give me a couple of different instructions and then always ask me: "You got this?" Obviously, I did not, because when she came back from work, I forgot half of the instructions, and the other half I did wrong. Why? Because I was only half awake!

> *Unless you fuel this moment with all*
> *you got, you will only absorb half of it.*
> *What you give is what you get.*

When I was at university, I went through a period where I was tired all the time. I woke up tired and I went to bed tired. My days were a bit of a haze, and I felt numb to my core. I was probably depressed, because I had no idea how to interact in a school with 17,000 students, where I had no sense of self and I felt I was invisible to the world.

Regardless of the reason, I remember how chaotic my day could become. One time, my teacher of Comparative Literature lent me a book, and I lost it three times in ten days! First I left it in the cafeteria, the second time it was on a table in the gardens and the third time I left it on top of the ATM machine.

My teacher freaked out, since every time the book was found it would get delivered back to him. He asked me if I was happy, and if I was really doing what I wanted to do. He told me he didn't see me engaged with anything at all, and that I was a ghost in my own existence. I told him to piss off. I was fine. I loved my life and I was fully in it. I left enraged and seriously frustrated.

"What is wrong with him? Who does he think he is? What gives him the right to tell me that? He can go and shove a ghost up his ass. He doesn't know me. I am fine. I AM FINE."

I justified my rage and didn't see how in denial I was of literally being a walking corpse.

Needless to say, I flunked the class.

Needless to say, he was totally right.

IT'S JUST A HABIT

Are you still in denial at this point, thinking why on Earth did you buy this book in the first place? I suggest you go for a walk.

Put the book down slowly – or throw it, it won't break – and go live your life for a while. Are you really whole-ass? Do you really give your all to the people your love? Do you say yes to life?

Our inability to change usually comes from the denial of the issue.

You can't change what you can't see.

If, on the other hand, you are intrigued to know if you are half-ass, this chapter will help you identify it, so that you can move towards a whole-ass life.

Here is the great news about being half-ass. Listen closely, and pretend I'm whispering you a secret:

It is only a habit.

And the magic of habits? They can change.

There is nothing wrong with you. There is nothing wrong with having learned to live life half here. It is one of the most common habits of humankind, and we can help the collective consciousness to break it. We can pass on a different way of life to the next generation.

It's not your parents' fault, your schools' fault, your society's fault or your culture's fault. It's definitely not the fault of whoever broke your heart! You are not victim to any circumstances.

Ultimately, we decide, either through
ignorance or wisdom, how we react to
the events that occur in our lives.

And this is great news as well, because it means you can change how you approach life.

TYPES OF HALF-ASS:

Identifying a half-ass is not an easy task. We can disguise it so well – I know I did. They come in different shades, flavors and colors.

In my adventures along the obscure and twisted paths of life, I've met, identified and tried on different types of half-asses. Hopefully, this list will help you highlight which way you tend to half-ass, if you ever do so.

In these descriptions, you will find:

- The motto they live by.

- The general approach to life of the specific type of ass.

- What triggers their half-assness.

Feel free to identify yourself with more than one, even though you will probably recognize that there is one that you constantly apply to your life more than the others. For me, I recognized different ones in different stages of my life.

> *Remember: you can't change what you can't see.*
> *Recognizing our habits is the first step*
> *towards changing them.*

And please, have fun with it. You need to start taking yourself less seriously. We are all going to die anyway, so you might as well enjoy life while you have it!

ASSES DIRECTORY

ANAL-ASS

(__ * __)

"I need to analyze this."

There are just too many choices, too many options and too much of everything. You tend to spend a lot of time analyzing every possible angle in order to make a decision. You weigh every single decision, trying to make absolutely sure that the decision you are taking is the correct one.

It´s not that anal-ass is confused, it´s just that you want to make absolutely sure that your decision is the right one in order to move forward.

Even deciding between restaurants is a pickle for you! You have pending projects everywhere around you, because you are trying to get clear on every single thing. You need to have your entire stream of thought flowing in one direction before you make a move.

I have a friend like this. He didn't postpone because he was lazy, he postponed because he still was thinking about it. He thought and thought and thought. Buying something off the Internet took him, like, three weeks of research, and then he would set it aside and resolve the issue two months later. Eventually, he would buy it. Or not. And more than once he missed the boat because the item was out of stock.

Mainly, he didn't want to make mistakes, but he ended up half-assing a lot.

> Triggers:
> When you have a deadline
> to make a decision.
> (__*__)
> When you don't have enough
> information to move forward, and
> the decision seems very important.

BAD-ASS

(♯▼Ⅲ▼)

"Next!"

You live life full on. You go about doing stuff all the time. You do this, and then that and then something else. You eat the world. You are bad-ass. There is no way you can be half-ass.

However, you long for steadiness, for a strong anchor that balances you out. You lack direction and purpose. You are full on in your external world, but not so much on the inside. You're like an ADHD kid on crack, jumping from one thing to another and never following through on one single thing.

That's not being whole-ass, dear. That's being half- ass on many things.

Took me a decade of commitment to my inner path to beat this one. No one could tell I was half-ass, but I certainly was. I was half-ass towards my heart's greatest desire; always uncommitted to every single thing that was placed in front of me, and always leaving things halfway done because I wasn't feeling full on about them anymore.

How can you whole-ass anything if you are already thinking all the ways you can get out of it?

You tend to always have a back door, a plan B, in life and in relationships. You have candles lit here and there, just in case the current thing doesn't work out. You seem to be giving it all, but deep, deep down you know that you have a huge reach, and what seems to another person as giving a lot, to you it's only giving the appetizer.

Triggers:
The possibility of falling into
a steady, secure life.
(♯▼Ⅲ▼)
When the thing you were so excited about
doesn't excite you that much anymore.

BUSY-ASS

"I can't, I'm busy."

"OMG, I am, like, so busy all the time." I don't know why, but I imagine an American woman when I think about this type. Busy, busy, busy. Wake up busy with so much shit to do; busy all day and busy all the time. Everything has to be done by appointment, and people are lucky if they find a spot in your schedule this week. You are *so* busy.

What you probably don't see is that a lot of your busyness comes from your own need to be busy, and to not stop and see beyond yourself. You might whole-ass your work, your gym and your appointments, but do you whole-ass your family life? What about time for yourself, or your passions, your hobbies and your sleeping time?

You are probably burnt out and wishing so much for a good vacation. When you are finally having a piña colada at the resort of your choice, you begin to feel so anxious with your time off that you end up using all your 'vacation' time organizing your next year's work schedule. Everything needs to be within your control.

You don't know how to stop, and you are afraid to learn how because you might discover that you have been experiencing inertia for a long while.

You can't be whole-ass in your life if you don't leave space for the unexpected.

Triggers:

When you have to change courses
due to unexpected situations.

(ₒⱯₒ = = |ᵐ ₸∴ą)

When you have to spend a
weekend without your phone.

COOL-ASS

(-▨|▨)

"It's just not cool."

Let's face it, you are cool. You dress cool, you act cool, you speak cool and you surround yourself with cool people. You are coolness incarnated, but cool gets in the way of, well, whatever doesn't look cool.

If it's not cool in the eyes of others or if it doesn't match your coolness code, you don't do it.

God forbid that you should fall into cheesy lines and public displays of affection. Hopefully your significant other won't spread a big mush on social media. How uncool! Being vulnerable? How uncool. Crying over a sunset? How uncool. Going to a mainstream place? How uncool. Listening to Justin Bieber? How uncool. Imagine if people knew that you listen to him when you're on your own, and even dance to Sorry.

You defend your cool more than you defend your right to breathe. You only surround yourself with cool people, and God forbid you are ever seen with uncool, common beings. You have a long list of uncool things that you won't do, like use a silly filter on Snapchat, because how immature! But deep down, you are terrified of showing yourself exactly as you are and being judged.

You are too cool to whole-ass.

Triggers:

When something embarrasses you.

(˗▨|▨)

When the real you is exposed.

DRAMA QUEEN-ASS

(~ | ´~;)

"What about ME?"

Between you and me, let´s face it, the world owes you. You are a queen, or a king, and this planet does not know what it´s got.

When things don´t go your way, you explode and throw tantrums. Why can´t they see that you are IT?

How does this affect your ability to whole-ass? Well, you only do it if people keep you happy. The moment things do not go your way, you resist doing what is needed.

When someone has a problem or something happens, instead of actually showing up fully for the person or circumstance, your first thought is how it makes YOU feel.

It is possible that you didn´t go to a party once, or maybe even many times, or lost a project you were eager to do because drama kicked in. You will not budge and you will not show them that you care. They have to live with the absence of you marvelous self. They are all stupid really. And you? Well, you end up half-assing one more thing.

You never feel understood. Your every need must be satisfied in the moment, and when the other person doesn´t get that, or doesn´t get you, all hell breaks loose. It´s hard for you to ask for forgiveness, or to let the drama go without a second thought. You drag up the past constantly, and always bring that shit into the present. You feel misunderstood and unsupported. They do not understand how they are making YOU feel. It's all about YOU. No one in the world gets you.

Triggers:

When you seem to be left out of the picture.

♛

(~ |'~;)

When you feel unfairly treated.

DUMB-ASS

(_?_)

"Errrr.... I don't know."

Your ass is basically confused.

You have learned that it is really easy to get away with anything if you just don't have a clue. It is not that you are avoiding life, you simply don't know. Why would you leap for something if you don't know? You spend a lot of time with your doubts, not knowing what you want or what the right step is, and getting more confused as time goes by.

Many times, you miss the window of opportunity because you can never quite come to grips with a choice. You just don't know, and you won't move until you that changes.

You don't know if you really like the person you are dating. You don't know if you want to marry your partner. You don't know if it's going to work out; you like that person but you just don't know. Your friend needed some help, but you just didn't know if you should've called or not. You probably constantly create a third person out there, just to justify your confusion. You don't know if you feel the same way anymore.

You don't really know if you like your job or how long will you follow that career path. How can you know if you can't read the future? Nobody really knows what's going to happen, so is it really your fault? You are actually being smart.

Triggers:

When you are faced with
making a long commitment.
(_?_)
When you have to choose a path.

FLAT-ASS

(_._)

"It's all so boring."

Life is flat. There is nothing to do. It's boring. Lame. Dull. Life sucks. Why would you even bother to whole-ass this pathetic existence? Your bohemian, pessimistic view of the world, by definition, impedes your ability to whole-ass anything, because there is a risk you might start enjoying life.

You are a mixture of '90s MTV character Daria, and a French aristocrat bored with life. Why are people so entertained by this dull planet, filled with nothing interesting? It's not that you are half-ass, it's that the world doesn't deserve your attention.

The only time you surround yourself with other humans is when they share your bored-faced, flat-assed view of life. You are like an emo that grew up without getting the memo that your teenage years have passed, and now it's time to engage life and be happy again.

You don't whole-ass because what's the point? It's all extremely boring, and we are all going to die anyway.

Triggers:
When you encounter someone
active and happy in their lives.
(_._)
When you have to enjoy something.

LAZY-ASS

(_(:3」 ∠)_)

"I'll get on it... soon."

You are not really half-ass, you just haven't found the right time yet! There are many things you want to do, and you will do them once the time is right.

But the time is never right, so you keep doing this mediocre thing you have to do, while you wait for that time when you will be full on with your dreams.

One day! One day you will show the world your abilities, but for now, you will just focus on all these tedious things you have to do before you take the big leap.

You tend to leave conversations, decisions and actions for later. Now is not the time to evaluate your dodgy relationship; now is not the time to face that issue that keeps coming up with a certain co-worker; now is not the time to call your mother to tell her you love her. You will do it later.

You make all these plans that one day, when the weather allows it, or when someone discovers you, and you've fixed everything else first, you'll execute. Postponement kicks your ass.

Triggers:
When you feel overwhelmed by
all the things you have to do.
(_(:3」∠)_)
When you realize all the steps you actually need
to take to achieve your dreams.

MOODY-ASS

(∩_∩)

"I am not feeling it."

First, you need to feel right about things. Your emotions need to be in order and you need to feel motivated. You need to sense and feel how the idea sits with you. The problem is that sometimes you wait and wait and wait until your emotions are in the right place. You wait for inspiration in order to act. You miss out the part where motion enables motivation.

You are so dependent on your moods that your life becomes a rollercoaster.

You give when you feel like it. Why would you give if you are not in the mood? When you are in a happy place, it all flows nicely, but as a poor sensitive child of the universe, you have to carry the burden of your moods, and so does everyone around you.

You waste a lot of time trying to get in the mood to do something. Maybe you get so excited about a project, start it, and then two days later wake up feeling like crap – energy stuck in your chest, feelings of depression, you name it. So, it takes you however many days to explore this feeling and to fix and get rid of it.

Once you are back to feeling good, maybe you will go return to the project, or maybe you'll be in the mood for something different.

But life is an ensemble, and the world can't wait for you to *feel* it. I learned that in acting school. My teacher would laugh at me if I gave her that excuse! "You better find a way to feel it now," she'd say. And I did.

Triggers:

When your emotions are not in place.

(∩_∩)

When a situation makes you feel uncomfortable, nervous or fearful.

NEW AGE-ASS

(_✿|✿_)

"It's all perfect."

Mercury must be in retrograde, because there is a wave of spiritual-yogi-unicorn-planet-angel people out there that all have something in common: they tend to half-ass using the universe as an excuse.

Maybe the planets are not being benevolent lately, so you might as well wait for Venus to be on your side. Or you read this month's planetary energy report in your spiritual blog of preference, and then cross-referenced it with two others, just to be on the safe side, and decided it's better to wait until the energies are in your favor. Soon, oh so soon, Earth will fall into the fifth dimension, and you'd rather wait until we are in a different reality where we all rise up in consciousness, instead of rising up yourself right now.

For you, every chakra needs to be in the right place.

You won't do something unless you feel only good vibrations about it, and it gives you positive, happy thoughts. You'll only engage in situations that give you a nice flow, and do not trigger any internal conflicts. Your unconditional love concept prefers not to have labels, because they're just so limiting.

What you do not tend to see is how you're missing out on a big chunk of opportunities for growth by avoiding them and not committing. The Universe responds to your energy, not vice versa.

You are so spiritual that you think your shit don't stink. When you attend one of hundreds of workshops and therapy sessions, or go to listen to a guru, you tend to immediately know who each piece of wisdom applies to, and how you are going to pass it on to them. Your friends and family definitely need help, but the advice seldom applies to you because... well, you are so spiritual already.

You probably spend more money on healing your past lives and getting future readings than you do on investing in how to live fully in the now.

If the Oracle said it, it must be true.

Triggers:
When you have to do something mundane.
(_✿l✿_)
When you have to face your own shit.

SICK-ASS

(_x_)

"I would, but my body might not let me."

Your body doesn't let you do what you want to do. You have a certain condition/disease aversion, and it's constantly getting in the way of you being full on. You'd rather stay in bed, you'd rather not show your muffin top and you'd rather not attempt to take that trip. What if your condition stops you?

You have a very violent relationship with your body. You know all its flaws, all the things that need fixing, and you would take that shirt off only if you didn't have those freckles in your back.

I know many wonderful people with hardcore conditions who are never stopped by them. Just yesterday, a dear, dear friend passed away after living with cancer and beating its ass a few times over the years. Only six weeks ago, we were hanging out together on the Greek island of Patmos. Believe me, it is not easy to get there! She even added a couple of days in Turkey prior to our retreat in Patmos, and then she was off to France. And just a month before, her daughter got married, and that took a lot of planning. She even prepared a flash mob for the party! She was a warrior, and pain never stopped her from living with a huge smile on her face, or kicking some ass along the way.

Sick-ass, you tend to want a lot of attention. Whenever you don't want to do something, face something or compromise on something, you pull the condition card. You are not half-ass; your body just always decides to break down at the perfect moment!

Triggers:
When something doesn't feel
right in your body.
(_x_)
Situations that make you feel self-conscious
about your image.

SMART-ASS

(_e=mC2_)

"Let me tell you why..."

"Let me explain to you the 100 well-founded reasons I have to justify the fact that I am not living up to my greatest potential." Your brain is too smart for your own good. You give serious thought and energy to convince yourself, and others, as to why you are not living it up, and you truly believe you are right.

This is one of the toughest types, and it can take a good ol' smack in the head to shake it off and open up to a different viewpoint.

Your head computes information and makes associations really fast, and it is so easy for you to justify every action or lack thereof. You are so smart, and you actually feel good when you come up with brilliant excuses for absolutely everything. Your belief systems are unshakeable, and nothing can break through the fortress of your mind; that is until shit breaks loose, and you are forced to change your concepts or perish.

Your type is the hardest one to argue with. Every action is justified by myriads of well-designed arguments. It takes a really strong counterpart to identify the bullshit behind. It's hard to see you are half-ass when you are always right!

Triggers:
When you feel attacked.
(_e=mC2_)
When you feel that someone
is telling you what to do.

PERFECT-ASSED

"Why can't people simply do things the right way?"

Everything needs to be perfect, but you keep mising the rights because you are focusng on the wrongs.

You have probably already noticed that "Perfect Assed" does not follow the proper alphabetical order. It is the only type of "ass" that is called "assed," and there are a couple of typos in the first paragraph. And no, you don't get an emojicon because it probably will be the wrong one for you, anyway.

You constantly wonder why can't people do things in the correct way, and believe that you have to do everything yourself if you want things to be done right.

It is common that you are not a good team player. You get annoyed and frustrated if things are not done the right way, and people might feel tense around you and your frowning forehead.

And while it's OK to be a perfectionist, this trait might keep you in the half-assed field because you don't allow yourself to do things, or work with others, unless you absolutely make sure that they are absolutely perfect.

The thing is, what you consider perfect might not be what others consider to be perfect. Perfection is in the eyes of the observer.

Daring to fuck up? You? Never!

Triggers:
When you do something
wrong and you can't fix it.

When you are forced to work with others
who you know are not perfectionists.

SORRY-ASS

"Why is this happening to me?"

You are a victim of circumstances. You live halfway not because you want to, but because life is constantly putting you in positions you don't really want to be in, and your hands, arms and ass are tied.

There seems to be some impending doom in the atmosphere whenever you're around. You always seem to fuck up, or feel as though you've already fucked up. As much as you try, life just seems to be mean to you. People don't understand that your role in this life is being a victim. Maybe you serve as a rug for others to walk over, and that is your lot in this lifetime. You'd rather apologize first, for everything. You are going to have to do it eventually, so why wait?

Triggers:
When you feel you stepped on
someone else's toes.
(‿|‿)
When you are told off or you
clearly made a mistake.

SUCK-ASS

:P(_*_)

"I don't want to disappoint anybody."

You want people to like you. You need to fit in. Who you are and what you do or don't do are based on this premise, so you can't whole-ass your life unless the people around you accept it.

If it's not your family, it's your partner, your social circle or your boss. It's so hard to keep them all happy! There are many occasions where you refrain from being yourself, being truthful or doing what you want because you'd rather be liked. It takes so much energy and juggling to maintain peace around you.

You don't do things that could potentially make you stand out. What if you are judged and exiled? Sometimes you wish you could do certain things, like be different or a bit more of a rebel, but you don't follow through. It freezes you not to be loved, and then you blame it on everyone else. When you don't do something that you want to, you end up feeling bitter and resentful.

You act in order to be liked and loved. You are never truly yourself, always trying to play one step ahead and second-guess what other people want. You have high expectations of acceptance and, ironically, it through this that you create a lot of non-acceptance for yourself.

You become like silly putty, adjusting constantly to what you think other people want, because deep down you don't believe the world will like you just the way you are. Silly!

Triggers:

When you can't please everyone in the room.

:P(_*_)

When someone clearly states that they don't like you or that they disapprove of you.

(UP)TIGHT-ASS

(!)

"What will other people think?"

"Oh, behave!" Be correct. Don't act silly. Don't say inappropriate things. Don't lose your temper in public. We don't do this kind of behavior in front of others, young lady!

You experience life as seen through other people's eyes, looking into you. How will it look? What will they say or think? What if they don't approve? You spend a lot of time considering how your actions might be perceived by your outside world, although your assumptions are probably wrong about 95% of the time.

You are so terrified about what other people think that it stops you from doing/saying/experiencing many, many things. God forbid you become an embarrassment!

Maintaining an impeccable image is more important to you than your soul's desires. It might be the barometer you even use to choose the people you hang out with, your partner, the jobs you settle for, for years, and the day-to-day activities you engage in.

The irony is that because you care way too much about what others think, you appear to attract a lot of judgement. It makes you feel like you want to hide under the table when someone says an unfiltered comment, or exposes one of your traits in front of others.

Social etiquette is so important, why can't people just behave properly?

But the thing is, my darling, that you cannot discover who you really are – therefore be whole-ass - until you stop caring so much what other people think of you and what you believe is socially expected.

Triggers:

When something you do is
taken the wrong way.
(!)
When you find yourself in the middle
of an embarrassing situation.

WEIRD-ASS

"I am not normal."

You are weird. Everything is weird. Your life is weird. People are weird. Too much weirdness in the world paralyzes you, yet it is your own weirdness that propels you. You tend to not spend too much time with people because there are only too many hours you can hide your weirdness.

Too normal makes you hesitate, and you wouldn't dare to embark on any activities that you'd seen depicted in the guidebooks of normality. You like being weird, and no one is going to take it away from you. Besides, if the world wasn't so weird, you probably wouldn't need to be this weird, either.

Maybe you avoid many encounters and activities because "fuck normal!" No one is taking your originality away from you, and you're not going to wear a normal dress to a wedding just because your mother asked you to.

Weird music, weird movies, weird attires and weird food. The thing is, sometimes you choose things not because you like them, but because they are weird. The potential for half-assing lies in the possibility that sometimes you might need to accept normal standards to get where you are going. Life doesn't look one certain way all the time.

Triggers:

When you are faced with normality.

(͜◌ | ◌͜)

When you are asked to do things
that everyone else does.

WISE-ASS

(_o^^o_)

"Yeah, Yeah... I know."

You know everything. You know how the world works, how people are and how life will turn out. And you definitely know what the neighbor is going to say the next time you invite her to a party.

Your life is one big loop of righteous same-same, and all because you *know*. And like a self-fulfilling prophecy, since you know it all, there is no room for life to throw up anything different.

It´s possible that you are highly intelligent, but it is still easy for you to jump to conclusions. The big problem is that your level of innocence is zero. You half-ass because you already know what´s going to happen, so why do it? The world to you is one big predictable event, where you are the fountain of all knowledge. It is possible that the people around you don´t like to discuss things with you because it is time wasted, given the fact that you already know.

You don´t offer anything different. You don´t try different ways of getting somewhere, and it´s really hard for you to learn new things or see new perspectives, because you just know.

Triggers:
When people talk like they know.
(_o^^o_)
When you are faced with a situation in which you
need to listen to other people's truth.

There you have it.

Were you able to identify with one, or maybe with several? Were you able to laugh at yourself after recognizing the common threads in your life? It's funny, isn't it! We think we are so unique, and then we realize we are just acting out an archetype.

Fantastic! Keep your habits in mind while we move on to the next stage, and be very aware of the thoughts or excuses that come up while we explore. Maybe it's just your half-ass habit!

Now that we have established the basis of half-assness, we can move to a much more exciting, full on road: Whole-ass.

Being whole-ass, as previously mentioned, is a habit that anyone can develop. All it takes is a desire to change.

Before I started writing this book, I was having a conversation with my boyfriend about it – he is my writing coach as well as my boyfriend – and he asked me, 'What do you want to write about?'

'Well, whole-ass!' I said.

'And how do you intend to fill out pages of content and make it into an actual book? What does a whole-ass person actually look like? What are their traits?'

'Hmm... good question.'

So, I embarked upon a dissection of the most common qualities I've observed in every whole-asser I've ever known. What is it that makes someone whole-ass their life? What do they all have in common?

The following chapters describe the main qualities required to be full on, with some suggestions to help you start embracing these habits in your own life.

I recommend not skipping any steps. Just imagine that you are exploring different aspects of yourself that already exist. All you need to do is find them, oil them and then make them a part of your everyday life, so that they become your default setting.

PART 2

WHOLE-ASS

"When the final curtain goes down, wouldn't it feel great to know that you lived your life completely?"

Dharma Raj Ishaya

Chapter 3

CLARITY

Get your ass in gear

Would you rather swim in a clear pool or a murky one? I don't know about you, but I prefer the first option. I also prefer a clear mirror over seeing my reflection in those wonky ones that you find at the circus.

Clarity is the first quality required to be whole-ass. Why? Because it becomes easier to know what to give your heart to.

Have you ever had to give all your time and energy to something you were not invested in?

During one of my many adventures through university, I knew I wanted to study something art-related, either writing or acting. However, I had so many preconceived ideas in my head about doing well in life, and being successful and productive, that in order to not freak my parents out, I decided to study engineering. I know, WTF?

God, it felt like I was in prison. Everything started becoming heavy: my body, my mind and my emotions – even the colors of life looked dull. It was a miserable time, and eventually I had to go for what I wanted, even if it meant changing my field of study one more time.

Many times, we try to be whole-ass towards something or someone that we don't really want in our hearts, and this is recipe for disaster and potential heartache.

There are two aspects to clarity: inner clarity and outer clarity. One cannot exist without the other. To put it another way, one is useless without the other.

> Pretend that here is quoted
> the beginning of a very
> famous song, sang by five
> British women in the 90's. If
> you still don't know, the song
> is called "Wannabe". Come
> on, just sing it in your head!

Being clear, first with ourselves and then with the world, can open the path to removing all rubbish and unnecessary experiences and setbacks on our road to a fulfilling life. It is the laying of the foundation for our own relationship with Truth, which is one of the main pillars of any blossoming endeavor in life.

Being true to yourself and to your world is the beginning. To be true, you first need to be clear.

WHAT DO YOU WANT?

The Spice Girls had no problem knowing and voicing what they wanted, what they really, really wanted. So lucky, those Spices! Most of us walk around not really knowing what we want. We are like antennas, attracting thousands of different signals that conflict with one another. We run around all day, every day, never stopping to ask one of life's most important questions:

What do I really want?

Imagine going out for a walk and expecting to find something specific, but not knowing what that something actually is. Yes, you might see many things, find funky shops and talk to some strangers; you might have a desire satiated by munching on a Montreal Smoked Meat Sandwich. But when you get back home, you'll have a feeling of dissatisfaction because you didn't find exactly what you were looking for.

How could you find it if you didn't know what it was in the first place? How could you possibly know which direction to take?

If the water is muddy,
the reflection will be unclear.

Imagine that your world, your universe, is here to serve you. It obeys every desire that you have. Every single one. However, it also obeys by delivering whatever doubts you have. If you are angry, it obeys by delivering things to be angry about. Guess what it will deliver if you are confused? You guessed right: confusion!

We have no real sense of how powerful we truly are. We are a source of infinite power, and if we really understood the power we hold, we would be very clear every step of the way.

For this chapter, at least, just pretend you are the master of the universe, and that everything you experience is a product of your thoughts and desires, whether conscious or hidden.

Hint: the people in your life are also part of your universe, and they also reflect where your inner self is at.

I don´t mean to scare you. I mean to give you a clearer understanding of what you are.

This is actually great news. See, if you are responsible for how the universe responds to you, and it´s easier to change yourself than to directly alter everything around you, this brings the responsibility back to you. You are not a victim.

I used to believe that I didn't like romance. I was this cool girl who was more like a guy, who liked to hang out with the boys. So, I wanted a type of *dudes'* relationship with my other half. At that point in my life, I was engaged to a guy with whom I had that type of relationship, but I always bitched and moaned at him about not being romantic, and constantly tried to change him.

Seven years ago, while out on a field trip during a six-month retreat in Spain, I was on a bus with my buddies. Four of us were talking, and one told this super romantic story about how he asked a girl to be his girlfriend. It was adorable. Then, the next one went on telling us about how her husband proposed to her.

Out of nowhere, I started crying like a baby. I completely saw how that was something I really wanted but didn´t get, mainly because I thought no one would ever feel that way about me! A voice saying, "No one will ever love me that way," passed through my head, and I was lucky enough to hear it. It was always there, unconscious, lingering, making me believe that I was unworthy of huge love. The people in my life were constantly responding to my expectations, and so whenever they were in my field, they didn't give me more because I didn't even believe in that possibility.

Sometimes we don't recognize what we really want because we don't believe ourselves worthy of it. So, we compromise. We settle for less. We would rather just accept whatever is being given to us.

> *It takes balls to discover what you want. To acknowledge it fully and not settle for less.*

If you are completely honest, like, really, really honest, what do you want? If you knew you could have absolutely anything in your life, what is it that makes your heart grow? What do you want in life more than anything?

PICK 'THE THING'

I want to live at the beach, but I also want to live in the mountains. I want ice cream, but I don't want the calories. I want a boyfriend, but I also want to be alone all the time. I want to be successful, but I don't want to work.

> *We want to live in the present moment, but we don't want to let go of the past or the future.*

Desires are natural to us. We often desire things, experiences and feelings. That is perfectly fine. However, sometimes we confuse the means with the goal.

For example, we desire a huge amount of money, but what we really want is to feel secure. We focus on the means instead of the desire itself. This can lead to a whole bunch of sidetracking.

We can want as many things as we please, but there is a common thread running through all of them: picking and sticking to one thing is much more powerful than wanting 100 different things.

What do you want?

What do you want more than anything?

What is it that you want to experience all the time?

What experience do you want to have? If every single one of your other desires were fulfilled, how would you feel?

HANDS ON ASS 1: THE THING.

Write down a list of things you want. Be honest, be real and be bold. It´s only for you, and no one will judge your choices.

Done? OK.

What did you come up with? A great job? A fulfilling relationship? A healthier body? Being less grumpy? Saving for some amazing shoes? Cleaning your home? Calling your parents everyday? Doing nice things?

How big or small the desire is doesn´t matter.

Now, take each of your answers and ask yourself the question, when I get this desire, how will it make me feel? What sensation would be left? It´s important that you do this.

There will probably be a common thread in all your answers. Happy? Secure? Peaceful? Joyful? Loved? Satisfied? Important? Fulfilled? The answer is not as important as the recognition of something. Usually, all the things we search for in life are pointing in ONE direction. ONE desire contains the rest of desires.

Identify that one desire. What is it that you want to experience the most in this life? What are you after?

> What is that desire that contains the rest of the desires?
>
> Write that ONE desire down.

Identifying what we want most in life is the first step towards clarity. This helps us by recognizing if we are pursuing certain things that are not even aligned with the greatest desire of our hearts.

When we are clear, there is a feeling of expansion, goodness and wellbeing. If you are honest, you know what you want. You do not need to try and find truth when it is already there. You just need to be willing to own it.

I am sure you have been through an experience in life where you have been faking something. It eats you up. You say *Yes*, but your insides are yelling *No*. You smile, but inside you are crying.

> ***When your inner clarity does not respond to your outer expression, constriction appears.***

BEING CLEAR IS AN EVERYDAY THING

Being consistently clear is not always an easy thing. We are such bundles of emotional ins and outs, and even though there are hundreds of opportunities every day to be clear, we do not always manage it. We have inherited years and years of passed-on generational concepts and beliefs that have clouded our clarity.

Here is one of the eternal crossroads that many couples and families encounter. If someone hasn't experienced a version of this conversation before, please email me immediately, as I would be really interested to know.

"What do you want to eat?"

"Whatever."

"Yeah, but where do you want to go for dinner?"

"I don't care – wherever."

"OK, how about that seafood place that just opened down the street?"

"Hmm... I am not really in the mood for seafood today."

"Well then, what do you want?"

"Whatever really..."

"Burgers?"

"No, I feel bloated."

"OK, then let's just stay home and make a salad."

"You never want to take me out."

Sound familiar?

My mom used to yell at my brother and me every Saturday when we pulled that crap. Not once did we not eat, because bless her, she loved us to her core, but man, try talking to a couple of teenagers on a Saturday afternoon, staring at the screen and playing Nintendo after a night out, and you will experience un-clarity at its best.

We all have different reasons or hidden beliefs that keep us from being clear.

A friend of mine has several funny stories about having to break up with girlfriends, like, four times because they didn't seem to get the memo. It's not that they were dumb, though. It's that he wasn't crystal clear. Perhaps, because there was a hidden fear of coming across as a total ass, he wanted to be a good guy and not hurt their feelings.

One day, with a huge look of surprise on his face, he told me: *"When you break up with someone, you actually need to say the words, 'We are over,' otherwise they do not get it."* I just started laughing, because I actually found it so endearing that he hadn't realized it before.

You have to be clear. It just makes everything simpler, easier and cleaner, and allows you to move on to a different place as quickly as possible.

Be clear when expressing what you want and what you don't want. Also, be open to the idea that when you voice it out loud, it might change.

**There is no use of being clear inside
if you are not clear outside.**

Clarity of who we are, clarity of speech and clarity of self brings relationships to a different level.

God, I hated being clear when I had emotions, especially the yucky, sticky ones. The ones that you know do not make sense, but will drown you if you don't voice them. I would have rather jumped out of a window and ran away very fast than simply been clear and transparent with the person beside me. I detested it.

There was a time where my walls were so high, and my positions so firm, that being clear when it came to how

I felt about things was not even a possible action in my universe. The first sign of a rush in the body would shut me down like an oyster, and keep me there, warm, fuzzy and alone.

I would cover the feeling up with every "It's OK!" I could find. I was always seeking unconditional love, and my misconception of what that meant led to me trying to be OK with everything everyone did. It was OK if they disappeared for days, slept with someone else or didn't say that they loved me for months. They must have been scared, and I had to be unconditional.

The "It's OK" would grow inside of me for weeks or even months, until I became so detached from the truth that I'd convince myself of 100 excuses why I should carry on with things as they were.

All of that drama because I couldn't open my mouth. So, forced to look at myself as the common thread in my own life, I saw it. It was painful, but I saw it. I was the one keeping myself separate from others. I was the one feeling isolated and misunderstood. How could I ever be understood if I would hide behind masks of "It's OK" and other arrogant facades?

"I am fine. I don't need you, so who cares?"

After the muddy moment, and that uncomfortable instant when I felt as if I was giving birth to a Gremlin, clarity started replacing muddiness, and a space was opened to allow the dynamics of my relationships to become different.

For the willingness to show myself as I was, the reward was that the universe reflected back more and more clarity every time. I started recognizing that the reasons why I felt misunderstood resided in my own reluctance to reveal myself.

I discovered that there are hundreds of people out there who don't expect me to be perfect. I discovered that it is OK to feel, and to show my colors and express myself. The more I became comfortable with it, the more comprehension I received back in return.

You don't have to be absolutely sure what will come out. The willingness to be clear can provide the space for confusion to transform into clarity.

Take it from me. I stutter, I mumble, I look around and I make weird sounds as a prelude to voicing what is happening inside. And as of right now, I am still alive, and every time it becomes easier.

HANDS ON ASS 2: CLEAR THE WHEEL.

Divide your life into different aspects:

Work life

Family life

Partner

Spirituality

Health

Social life

Finances

Emotions

You can add or remove aspects according to your own life. This is just an example.

Now, ask yourself the following questions, area by area. Write the answers down:

What do I really want from X area?

Am I being clear in regard to what I want?

If not, what is stopping me from being clear?

What can I do to start being clear? Write down separate steps for each area.

"We see in order to move;
We move in order to see."

William Gibson

CLARITY TRAPS

Each habit and trait has its own set of traps and blind spots, where we think we are using or embodying the trait, when in reality we are doing just the opposite. This section will highlight these traps, so that you can turn on the headlights and see straight into the eyes of these tricky raccoons.

I HAVE NEGATIVE THOUGHTS ABOUT IT

OK, so you know what you want, but then you experience doubts because you have negative thoughts about it.

"Oh, maybe I am not sure this is what I want. Maybe I didn't really want it in the first place, because if I did, I wouldn't have all these negative thoughts about it."

Dude, your head is like a crazy monkey. It tells you all the positive things about something, and then it tells you all the negative ones right after. Then, it lists the positives again, only to turn it all around the next minute.

If you are waiting for your head to speak to you coherently before being clear about what you want, you are basically screwed.

One of the reasons I was nicknamed Runaway Bride was because I wanted to run away every time shit hit the fan in a relationship. As soon as we hit a bump, my head would start going crazy, listing all the reasons why I didn't really even want to be in this relationship in the first place, why I don't need this crap and why I want to go NOW.

One time, I moved to a new city just a week after starting a relationship with a guy, who I'll call Music Man. Not only did I move to the same city as him, but also into the same house. What can I say? It was a bold move, but I was head over heels and finally enjoying the kind of romance that I'd starved myself of for so long. And it did last four years, so we must've done something right!

I did not know many people in the new city, and I had no real life of my own. We'd been dating, getting to know each other and living together for a month, and then one day we had this massive fight. I seriously cannot remember what it was about, but I do remember that I was frustrated to my core.

All my thoughts were telling me to get the hell out of there, how I hated all of this and that I didn't want to be in that, or any, relationship anymore.

"Take me to a hotel," I said. "Take me to a hotel now."

It was three in the morning.

"I am not taking you anywhere."

I didn't have a car of my own, so I couldn't just up and go. We lived in downtown Monterrey, Mexico, in the midst of the 2010 wave of violence, so walking or hailing a taxi was not an option.

"TAKE ME TO A HOTEL NOW. I WANT TO LEAVE NOW. I DON'T WANT TO BE IN THIS RELATIONSHIP ANYMORE." Yes, I was yelling.

You know what the *bastard* did? He started laughing at me, and then he told me it was just a fight, nothing more, and that shit going wrong for a while didn't mean anything.

That was the beginning of me discovering that my head always throws the same shit at me; the same old story. It wasn't original to this particular guy. It was the same story that my mind told me every time a relationship wasn't going the way I expected it to go.

So, no, negative thoughts are no indicator of not wanting something, as I clearly did want that relationship.

I still get the same streams of thought sometimes, two relationships removed from Music Man, and sometimes I even believe them. But every time you choose the truth instead of the common stories in your mind, the stories lose their power and believability. Now it's easier for me to recognize these thoughts as just the old story about how my relationship won't work.

If you are clear about something, and one day you have negative thoughts about it, GET OVER IT. Do whatever you need to in order to move past the *emo* stage.

> "Dealing with complexity is an inefficient and unnecessary waste of time, attention and mental energy. There is never any justification for things being complex when they could be simple."
>
> Edward de Bono

ATTRACTION TO COMPLEXITY

If you are of Generation X, you might be familiar with the name Troy Dyer. Ring a bell? No? I am talking about Ethan Hawke's character in the movie *Reality Bites* (1994). I was 13 when I saw it, and it rocked my pre-teen world. All those complex, intellectual, twisted, lost young adults just trying to get somewhere in life. Being complex and a little scruffy looked so cool!

Troy Dyer immediately became the epitome of the guy I was going to date when I grew up. Here is the best description of him, voiced out by Vickie, Winona's eccentric best friend in the movie:

"He's weird, he's strange, he's sloppy, he's a total nightmare for women... (I can't believe I haven't slept with him yet)."

If you are of an artistic nature, or if you grew up watching soap operas on TV, complexity is probably one of the biggest labels you define yourself with. Being complicated speaks to such depth of self.

However, complexity is *so* last season.

Clarity resides in simplicity.

This doesn't mean that you can't be a colorful person, full of tones and richness. It doesn't mean that you don't have depth, or that you can't experience life through all the pores of your being. That's not being complex. That's being human.

Despite the attraction of being contradictory; to be pushed and pulled, as by the gods' whims in a Greek tragedy; the tendency to be an over-thinker, over-feeler and over-everything else only serves to cloud clarity.

Embrace simplicity. You won't be less of a wonderful person; you'll be a colorful person with simplicity in your heart. This world is too complex as a result of complex human minds. This century is urging us to return to the simple.

Simple humans, simple world.

You might think you can't, but you can. Believe me, I have been there. I was born in a complex crib, and in my family, complexity defines who we are, especially the women. But even the patterns of our thinking process can be changed, as Edward de Bono has masterfully shown us again and again. If creativity and useful thinking can be learned, why not simplicity? It can be, of course.

I am lucky and blessed that I found a meditation practice, which is so ridiculously simple that even now, 12 years later, I am still marveling at how easy it makes my life. But more on that later.

Whole-ass people do not have time for complexity and its setbacks.

Simple is the new black.

JUST FLOW, DUDE

When I was 21, I became addicted to the spiritual, esoteric and new age. I loved anything that involved wearing white flowy dresses, going to meditation circles – which I didn't really get – attending all sorts of therapies while wearing crystals, and saying "Namaste" (or "In Lakesh", which is the Mayan equivalent).

There is nothing wrong with that lifestyle if it rings your bell, but for me, this whole "flow" thing was merely a great excuse not to get on with my life.

I've met a lot of hippie-chic kids in their late-20s, or even their 30s and 40s that are still "flowing." They're still living off and/or with their parents, and still don't have a clue what they want. They're just waiting for a signal from the universe. Why?

"Just flow, dude."

"I was just flowing, and I cheated on you."

"I was just flowing, and they cut my power off."

"I was just flowing, and now I'm pregnant at 18."

"I was just flowing, and I've arrived at the end of my life with no sense of fulfilling my purpose."

Flexibility is an amazing trait. Setting a goal, and then being open to the road looking different to how you believe it should, can save you from many headaches. Let's face it, things are going to go their own way no matter what.

But the point I am making here is that we sometimes fall into the trap of excusing our lack of clarity by applying the concept of flowing. You have to read it as if you are a 1970's dude, just heading out of Woodstock, perhaps really, really high. *"Just flow, dude."*

Speaking of high, I was a major stoner for, like, five years. As much as I don't want to reveal this to certain members of my family, it's true, and it's coming out of my fingers without me being able to stop it.

I loved the feeling of it. The high, the way single moments seemed to last an eternity and how my brain started looking at things from a different perspective. Oh, and the joy... the *joy!*

But after the novelty passed, and it stopped being this thing a group of friends did one summer to have fun, it became just another habit. A really enjoyable one, but a habit nevertheless, which at some point revealed itself to be more detrimental than positive.

I developed a less controlling self, and was more able to flow with certain things, mainly because weed has a way of making you not care about stuff, but at the same time I was numb. The drive to achieve something slowly faded from my energy field, and I could basically spend three days in a row just wandering around the flow of highness, away with the fairies, jumping around the realms of my imagination.

It started cutting me off from reality.

I could not see how long it took me to do anything! Eventually, all the practical things were piling up: banks, bills, dry cleaning and even picking up a package. For months – or was it years? – every responsibility was pushed back for another moment.

What I thought was being in an enhanced state of consciousness turned out to be chronic dullness, drifting and *flowing*, with no clarity whatsoever.

You don't have to be a stoner to suffer from the Stoner Syndrome, by the way.

I used to constantly have the following argument with Music Man:

He loved zoning out while watching TV. He did work a lot, and was definitely not one to be labeled as a *"flow, dude"* kind of guy, but he would often drift into this dead zone of binge-watching.

I kept explaining to him that being in this vegged-out state, where you basically numb yourself to the world, was not being at peace. There was nothing wrong with what he did, but he kept calling it "being present," and that really pushed my buttons, because it was the opposite of that! Being a brain-dead zombie is not the same as being present beyond any sense of limitation (the fact that I wasn't loving him exactly as he was is a totally different story).

The point is that sometimes we zone out and avoid ourselves, and keep trying to pretend that numbing our senses is the same as finding a real state of happiness. But if you have ever had a hangover, there is the proof that this is not the case. All the jolliness, happiness and sense of greatness that comes from a night of partying reveals itself to be a moral disaster once the effects wear off.

I am not trying to be a hypocrite here. I've partied massively in my time, and that's how I know that the false *flow* of drugs, alcohol and wonky concepts will only cloud clarity. Watch out for that one.

"You can wait for the stars to align, or you can commit and the stars will align for you."

Chapter 4

COMMITMENT

The mother of whole-asses

It seems to me that this is one of the scariest words of the 21-century. Commitment is becoming an alien concept that refers to an action people used to do, in the last century, mainly because they didn't have another option.

But now we have thousands of options for everything. Amazon is the modern merchant. Whenever possible, I order my coffee from Canada, as Kicking Horse Coffee is by far the most delicious cup of Joe to start my mornings. I shop for towels in Taiwan, I have Greek olive oil shots in the morning and with a click I hang out with my friends in the cyber world. Options are everywhere, and they are limitless.

I work online, so I do not even have to commit to going to an office or having a specific house in a specific place. I work wherever I am, and I love it. I have many freelancer friends that one day do one thing, and then the next day they change careers completely. It's now incredibly easy to jump around between jobs.

As you can see, I do take advantage of our new possibilities, and I love the freedom that comes with an ever-connected world. However, there is a downside: we have lost our ability to commit.

Why commit when there is always another thing around the corner? Why commit when with one message you can cancel? Even committing to a Saturday night plan is an old concept now. You better keep your options open, and if you wish to cancel, you can just send a WhatsApp.

Today, I read a few chapters of *Unhooked Generation* (2006), a brilliant book by Jillian Straus. She questions why our generation, Generation X, has so much trouble finding "the One," and looks at why we suck at marriage. It is a brilliant piece of work, and I think every person should read it. It presents a very true to life picture of all the things we do in order not to commit.

WHAT IS COMMITMENT ANYWAY?

I keep hearing here and there the expression "commitment issues." It is such a perfect excuse to not follow through with something. "I would go to the gym/ take that six-month workshop/eat that steak... but I have commitment issues."

Commitment is the act of saying YES to any experience, endeavor, task, path or person, and then keeping at it no matter how it goes, instead of only being interested when it seems to be working out and going your way.

> *Commitment is having*
> *no ifs, buts or howevers.*

You commit to an idea, and you have the willingness to do whatever it takes for it to happen, and stick with it after the initial emotion is long gone.

First clarity, then commitment.

You may be one of those people out there who truly knows what you want, but if you are not committed getting to it, you are fried. Clarity opens the path to delivery, and commitment lights up that path for the order to arrive at its rightful owner.

As you commit to your world and to your life, your world and your life will commit to you.

"The definition of the word commit is to "devote oneself unreservedly." This means holding absolutely nothing back; giving
100% of everything you've got. It means being willing to do whatever it takes for as long as it takes. This is the warrior's way.
No excuses, no ifs, no buts, not maybes
- and failure isn't an option."

T. Harv Eker

I used to be committed to being completely uncommitted. As you know, I never finished a degree and I bounced from one thing to another, and seldom committed myself to any relationship. Always, one of my feet was outside the door, with the shoe on, ready to start running. Therefore, nothing seemed fulfilling. How could something ever appear to be full if I was only seeing it with half of my heart?

In order to see reality complete, I needed to be there completely.

And I wasn't, and it wasn't intentional.

More than anything, I wanted freedom. It's been a burning desire since I was 13, and somewhere along the way, I assumed it meant that I needed to be free from my body. My first attempt to be free was popping a bottle of sleeping pills one random afternoon. Obviously, I didn't die, so 'Yei' for me.

Freedom was my quest, and I started assuming that in order to be really free, I needed to have no strings attached, no promises and no long-term leases. I assumed that commitment was the opposite of freedom, so I was really committed to being uncommitted.

As a complete rebel, the world was utter nonsense to me, so I decided that the only way to survive was to fight against everyone and everything. No systems, no common places, no social conventions and under no circumstance would I ever listen to authority. A social anarchist!

I was absolutely devoted to destroying anything that seemed like a tool to "normalize" people. I had no specific cause but my own. People should be free, and freedom meant no structures. Freedom meant not ever listening to what anyone else had to say because, well, they were mostly stupid. And I was faithful to that for a long, long time.

Being an extremely passionate person, my passion sometimes created chaos; inward chaos emotionally and mentally, and outward chaos, shaking structures in people and circumstances in a very aggressive way. My passion was all over the place, and so was I.

Even when I was a 26-year-old lass living in Barcelona, studying acting and living in the most wonderful neighborhood, El Born, with the best, most creative friends, and engaged to a lovely musician, the relationship had to be non-monogamous, because of course I didn't believe in commitment. Even though we never actually slept with other people, I felt better keeping my options open. My hunger for freedom kept me wanting more, kept me awake at night wondering what else I could do to scratch the itch, to feed the monster and to feel free. Where else could I go? What else could I change? What other things could I add? What other things could I get rid of?

I was extremely closed-minded, and at some point I had to even shut my heart out of business, so that I could actually lead a life of "freedom."

I was committed to my freedom, but looked at it from totally the wrong angle. I don't how I was able to walk around for so many years with my head between my knees.

I already practiced meditation, and even though I loved it and was kind of consistent with it, I never completely saw it as a path. But since my way didn't seem to be working at all, and Ascension –the meditation I practiced, which actually worked for me – was the only thing that I seemed to remain committed to throughout the years, I decided to give it a shot.

Luckily, one day, I met the coolest monk I've ever met in my life.

She walked through my door one January day in Barcelona, to teach a course that I had organized because my practice, Ishayas' Ascension, was virtually unknown in that town, and I needed meditation to keep me sane.

So, a couple of monks came over from England, ready to teach a course. I had no idea who was going to show up at my door, so I was delighted when one of them was a woman, young, cool and fun. Like, really fun. She stayed for, like, ten days, and the whole perspective of having an internal practice changed for me.

We talked about everything that existed under the stars, while also eating popcorn and watching *Sex and the City*. I could have the most profound conversation with her, and then the next moment pull the most smart-ass comment about the lamest thing, and we would start laughing like little kids.

I fell in love, and being around her was a constant experience of bliss. She had something I wanted. I couldn't put my finger on what it was, but I really wanted it. She was a much happier, *freer*, version of me.

I never saw myself as a monk, or someone whose path was to lead a truly spiritual life because, well, I like to wake up late, I love meat, I do not like cold showers, I love sex and I curse a lot. Put all those in a martini shaker, agitate it and you will not come up with a Monk Special. At best, you will have made yourself a Dirty Monk with extra olives.

Turns out, it wasn't true, and Satta showed me how I had been confusing every single aspect of being spiritual with a bunch of concepts. Through her, I saw that commitment to freedom was an inward movement, that I needed to be free from the constructs of my own mind, and that a constant internal dedication to that freedom had nothing to do with how it looks on the outside world.

It still took me some years to actually commit fully, but that was the beginning of me straightening my back and walking tall, with my eyes properly set in the right direction.

Committing to the thing I want the most was the first step towards seeing my world transform into the most wonderful of adventures, where only joy, love and constant laughter fill my days. I would be lying if I told you that I don't have any challenges left, but my eternal commitment to my path makes it so easy to let go of any shit.

Commitment is not the opposite of freedom, *au contraire mes amies*. Being uncommitted is never going to lead to a full on life. It will always reveal reality half-alive, so you are condemned to be dissatisfied with whatever life puts before you.

You can repeat this cycle forever, and all you'll get is a mediocre life until you see what is actually happening. It's not the options out there that suck. It's you being only half-assed committed that sucks.

How you do one thing
is how you do everything.
How you do one thing
is how you do everything.
How you do one thing
is how you do everything.
How you do one thing
is how you do everything.
How you do one thing
is how you do everything.
How you do one thing
is how you do everything.

HOW YOU DO ONE THING IS HOW YOU DO EVERYTHING

Read that statement many times. Grab a notebook and repeat it as if you were a child.

If only you grab these 10 words from this book, and recognize the truth behind them, your life will probably change.

I hated it.

One of my friends has a t-shirt that states, *"The truth will set you free, but first it will piss you off."* This quote belongs to Gloria Steinem, and even though I do not consider myself a feminist, that quote applied perfectly when it came to my dynamic with this statement. The first time I heard it, it came from my Teacher, Maharishi Krishnananda Ishaya, the coolest, most conscious, Ducati-riding being in the whole universe. I do not remember what the conversation was about, but he told me:

"Maharani, how you do one thing is how you do everything. Do you believe that statement?"

I heard a *screeeeech* in my head, and the little mouse that lives inside started looking over every single folder, trying to compute while scratching its tiny head.

"Hmm..." I wanted to say no, as that would be disastrous! *"... Really?"*

"Oh, yes."

(dead silence)

As I wrote those lines, I actually sat for a while and let that statement sit with me again. It's so true! In terms of commitment, if you are half-assed about something, you are probably half-ass about everything.

If you bail and avoid a situation when you do not like what is happening, you probably do the same in every other aspect of your life.

If you tend to blame people in one area and are not willing to take on suggestions, you probably do it in every other area, too.

If you give it all you've got, with no back door, in one area, then you probably live like that in all areas of your life!

Your world is not segmented or fractioned. We sometimes compartmentalize in order to organize our lives, and it can be really helpful, but when it comes to our experience of life, our whole world is a reflection of us; of who we are and what we believe; of what we resist and what we love.

The way you approach one aspect of life is the same way you approach other areas, too.

In terms of being whole-ass, this is great news.

If you want to whole-ass your world, you just need to pick ONE thing; one thing to commit to fully, entirely, with all your heart, body and soul, and the other areas of your life will start matching. They will start rising to the occasion, all because you rose up, and there is no way that your world won't match your inner attitude.

That is also something I learned from my Teacher. In his eternal patience, he teaches me over and over again how to whole-ass my inner path, my path to freedom, so that I can have the most wonderful, marvelous, free, unbelievably blessed life, and be able to serve this world giving my best.

> "The GenX approach of 'keeping your options open,' or holding back from a complete commitment, is one of the biggest obstacles to finding true love today. Commitment isn't like a high- or low-risk investment. If you don't invest fully, you have no chance of reaping any reward.
>
> Many married couples have reminded me that marriage is a leap of faith, even in the best of circumstances. There are no guarantees; there are no money-back returns.
>
> By failing to fully commit, many of us cheat ourselves out of the kind of depth we long for in a relationship. Over and over, the couples with successful relationships told me how their unions transformed them, once they fully committed."
>
> Straus (2006)

This extract is from Jillian's book, and even if in this case it refers to marriage, it applies everywhere else as well. Anything transforms once we fully commit to it. We start to enjoy it, to get the juice out of it; we start to see the aspects of ourselves that are not committed, and we can, hopefully, let them go.

The first 100% committed relationship I had started six years ago. I knew, even before I met him, that I wanted to learn how to experience a full on, committed relationship. I saw that the only way to experience unconditional love was if I committed fully to the person in front of me. I had the sense that I had a lot of shit getting in the way, such as concepts, beliefs, attitudes, whiny voices and a wandering eye. But I really wanted to experience it, and I knew that this was the only way.

How could I be committed to my spiritual path if I kept having half-ass relationships?

The universe delivered exactly the right person to experience this with: Music Man. I was very clear from the beginning. I told him I was in it 200%, and that I wanted the same in return. I expressed that I wasn't interested in cheating or being unfaithful to this new relationship.

For the first time, I was clear. That was the first thing I did differently.

He wanted to play that way, too, and he went all the way with me. I had recently moved back to Mexico and was spending some time at the beach, in what was my first attempt at writing a book. He came to see me there, and that's when we began our relationship. He asked me to move in with him, so I did.

I remember the first day I was at his house. It was the middle of August, 40 degrees outside, he had gone to work, and I didn't dare to even turn the AC on. I started freaking out. My head was going a million miles an hour and my breath was shortened. I kept looking around, not recognizing anything there, not knowing if that could be my home and doubting if I actually felt for him what I thought I felt.

In that moment, my mother called me. Usually, mothers carry the judgmental voice and are the Jiminy Crickets on our lives, but this time she wasn't. Her voice soothed me. She started laughing at me and what I had done, but in a loving way. She told me it was good for me to have the intention to go for it and to put all my eggs in one basket. She was happy I was in love. It also helped that Music Man had sent her an email, telling her how happy he was and what an awesome daughter she'd raised.

So, with my mother's blessing, I committed to being there and giving it my all, no matter what.

It wasn't the easiest of relationships, but we were both very much in love and very much committed. Every single reason why I didn't want to commit came up. Every single thing that could make me cringe, resist, fight, reject, feel victimized or unloved came up during those years.

All of my preconceptions about marriage, monogamy, independence and femininity were brought to the surface. Sometimes he played the knight, sometimes the butcher, and I am deeply and eternally grateful to him for having played his part to the fullest. I honor everything he taught me, and appreciate him for showing me that I am much more than I realized, and that I carry the ability to love with all my being. I had to see my own shit front row, to see everything that was keeping me in separation, unwilling to give myself fully, before I could let it go.

The only reason I was able to do that was because I committed fully without waiting until when, or if, I knew he was right, or the One. For better or worse, from the very first moment I committed as if it were the real thing, and it was. We experienced absolutely everything we had to; we didn't leave any unresolved business, and we tried every single color in the universe to make the relationship survive over time. When we broke up, there was nothing else to do and nothing more to give, and the love remains forever untouched.

> **You can call it a great game when**
> **you know you gave it all.**

As my dad told me, "You didn't have a failed relationship. You had a successful relationship that arrived at its end."

It's my personal belief that relationships are a great barometer for measuring if we are whole-ass or not. We tend to be uncommitted and to have a back door open. It makes sense, as we do not want to get hurt, and we don't know how to do this without putting our armor on. But it's worth a try. It's worth $1 million to learn to be completely all in, whatever it takes.

HANDS ON ASS 3: THE ONE.

Grab the wheel where you described all areas of your life. Rate each one from 1 to 10 in terms of how committed you are, 1 being 'total half-ass' and 10 being 'whole-ass'. Are there any patterns? Do most of them fall into a similar category of numbers?

Now pick the one that inspires you the most to give 100%, whatever it takes. Do not worry about bringing the rest to a higher number, even if you discovered they are very low.

Focus on ONE. One thing to commit fully to. Do it consistently and consciously.

If it helps, write down steps and actions to be more committed. Seize the opportunities that will naturally present themselves once you've made an inner commitment.

Trust me, the rest will follow.

WHATEVER IT TAKES

How badly do you want what you want?

Are you committed **to doing** whatever it takes?

Are you willing **to let go** of whatever it takes?

Are you willing **to be open** to whatever it takes?

Are you willing **to risk** whatever it takes?

You need to want it with all your heart, body and soul, with an attitude of "whatever it takes!" That's what commitment is; it is an inward action. It's an internal attitude that with practice becomes the default platform on which you build your life.

Imagine that a committed heart is a laser, and wherever you direct it, it sends its full power there. It wouldn't work the same if, instead of a laser, your heart was a fickle keychain lantern, would it? Learning to have a heart on fire is one of the most important things we can do to lead a whole-ass life. A heart that is a lighthouse, always illuminating your path to happiness.

What is that which creates a burning feeling in your heart – that willingness to do whatever it takes, no matter what? Go for that.

It is only when we go after it that we start seeing everything that gets in the way, and because we want the thing so much, we gain the ability to keep walking forwards, no matter what stands before us. But remember, if you commit to that one thing, regardless of how many setbacks you encounter, or whatever your mind throws at you, it will benefit every other area of your life.

> "The Holy Spirit will go to
> any means to expand love."
>
> MSI. Rg Veda

We are vessels of absolute, pure, pristine love. The emptier the vessel, the more love and creation can come through us. The only way to whole-ass this life is by being the emptiest version of ourselves.

So, what do we do first? Clean the vessel, get rid of the rubbish, clear the trash – you get the idea. But it's a little difficult to clean a room when the lights are off, isn't it? If you walk into your garage at night, with the lights off, you might trip or hit your toe against a box on the floor, and any attempt to clean it will be a nightmare that will take you forever.

Commitment is switching the light on.
Then the rubbish starts revealing itself.

And then, it's just a matter of actually taking the trash out, instead of swimming in it and putting it back where it was,

I've seen many cases where people commit to something, only to get discouraged midway through because of all the stuff that happens, which "appear" to be obstacles on the road. What if they are not obstacles? What if they are just there to help you see your negative attitudes manifested, so that you can change them? What if they are helping you become more focused on what you actually want?

Remember, you're committed, whatever it takes.

Remember, shit WILL come up.
See it for what it is and keep walking.

COMMIT TO. COMMIT NOT TO.

Committing gives us a clean cut. No loose ends, no fake doors. We stop wasting our time in everything that is not in our interest, and we start filling our lives with what actually matters.

So, if you commit to doing something, do it. But also, when you don't want to do something, when you are clear that you don't want or you are done with one thing, commit to NOT doing it. Move on fast.

Earlier this year, during a meeting with our teacher at a retreat in Mexico, he talked to us about commitment in the context of relationships, and he said:

"If you are committed to being with someone, be. But also, if you guys are not together anymore, commit to not being together."

It blew my mind!! I saw a thread of many, many times where I would end a relationship but kept the door open, just a tiny bit, just in case I changed my mind, just in case I felt kinda bored or lonely one random afternoon.

And I did that with so many other things! Projects, housing, you name it.

I'd learned to commit fully to someone, but I hadn't considered the other side of the coin. I was so excited to see this as an opportunity to apply commitment and clarity to yet another area.

Commit every step of the way. It is your steps that exude commitment, and not the goal.

Walk with commitment wherever you are going. Be committed, both to what you do want and what you don't.

Once you are walking that way, then the game becomes something else.

Sometimes, it seems we believe that committing means not having a choice, and losing our freedom of election. Truth is, we do have a choice, we always have a choice, but choice comes to mean something different when we commit.

The old way goes like this: half-committing to something, jumping around between if you want to do this or not; if now you want to, now you don't; if you'd rather leave this because you don't like it anymore, or you'd rather not leave this because maybe you do like it now. (Man, I got tired even writing that). By committing, we put that to rest, saving ourselves lots of energy and mental chaos.

Once the commitment is done, fully, then choice resides within the context of that commitment. We choose between love and innocence, or fear, reject and resist; to expand, to see beyond what is limiting us and taking a leap, or to stay limited and constricted by choosing the old ways again.

Our choice becomes one of depth, instead of one of direction.

And then we are more aligned with a healthier way of being, a way of evolving that keeps propelling us to a be a constant torpedo of whole-assing yourself.

"Whenever a human being chooses for the old self-destructive behavior and thought patterns — the old grooves of limitation and lack — the evolution of life into perfection is slowed.

Whenever a human chooses for the ascending currents of praise, gratitude or love, life progresses with lightning speed into the indescribable beauty of the divine presence.

There is a choice in every moment for every human.

Go with judgment, with fear — or align with the holy spirit, with innocence, with love.

This is the purpose of human free will — to make the one choice that matters here, the one choice that heals, the one choice that is capable of permanently transforming a life to perfection and joy."

MSI

COMMITMENT TRAPS

SPLIT DESIRES

Committing to different desires can be more detrimental than beneficial when these desires act as opposing forces.

This is what Ishayas call split desires. You desire a happy life, but you also desire not to move out of your comfort zone. You desire peace, but you also desire to keep dwelling in the past constantly. You desire a healthy relationship but you also desire to keep your self-destructive patterns.

That's why it's so important to become aware of the patterns in our mind and the grooves that linger, ruling our everyday lives. No matter how clearly and consciously we desire something, the task is to learn that we can let go and unlearn every single self-sabotaging concept and belief.

That ONE desire comes in handy here. Committing to that desire with all your heart, body and soul avoids the trap of falling into split desires.

Let's say, for example, that your number one desire is PEACE. Commit to that. Commit to doing whatever it takes to experience peace in your life. Allow whatever is not peace to come to the surface so you can let it go.

Ask yourself this question in regard to any other desires you may have:

A great job or peace?

A relationship or peace?

Pizza or peace?

Success or peace?

It doesn't mean you won't get all of the others, but what it does mean is that all the others will start to align under the banner of peace. Anything you get will give you peace, and if you don't get it, you can be absolutely positive that it is because it wouldn't give you peace.

A split desire is like wanting a BMW and also never wanting to drive a car ever again. The universe thinks, *"Like, WTF?"* I mean, come on, we have to help it out a little! It attends to tons and tons of weird random desires every single day, so let's give the big guy a hand.

BACK DOOR. WHAT IF THE GRASS IS GREENER?

> *99% commitment is not 100%. 99% is the same as being not committed at all.*

Why? Because it means that the back door is still open. The emergency sign is still on, shining bright, reminding you constantly where the exit route is.

What does that create? Chatter in the mind, doubts, excuses; it keeps the game running, so you can be constantly trapped in analyzing and agonizing over your decision. You keep your eye open for signs that might help you see why this is such a bad idea, and there's quite a high chance that you'll talk yourself out of it.

I don't think anyone who has ever achieved a great thing in life was 99% committed to it. That 1% leftover is one of the biggest traps for staying half-ass forever.

If you were in a job interview, the job of your dreams, and you told your interviewer: "If you give me this job, I will be 99% in – 99% committed to this," do you think you would get it?

You have to blow up the back door.

Even though I am just an amateur, I love to play poker, Texas hold 'em, to be exact. For me, it's like playing an extreme sport. There is so much rush and adrenaline going through my body!

I suppose I suck at having a poker face, because when I know I have a winning hand, I get super excited. And what gives me the rushiest of rushes is when I go all-in. I don't know what is going to happen, I don't know if the other player will get all my money, but I know there is no way back.

Either you win or you lose, but you gave
it all, and there is no way back.

If you really want to taste what commitment feels like, you must destroy the concept of a back door once and for all.

This is why clarity is so important. You will start committing only to what makes you vibrate, what gives you electricity in your body, what excites you and what makes your heart sing. Having no back door means you will only move forwards. You will stop hesitating, and your steps through life will create a bigger echo.

Remember, once you have both feet in, things look different. The grass where you are standing suddenly seems greener, puffier, and flowers appear out of nowhere. It's your grass, you created it, and you learn to appreciate it as the best grass in town.

COMMITMENT CONTROL

Sometimes we try to control how our path unfolds.

We commit to something, but we want it to come at our pace, as and when we are ready. We attempt to control every single aspect of its delivery to us.

The universe's delivery system is set in motion once we commit. We don't know how it's going to happen, or how it's going to look, but trust me, it will.

However, many times our control mechanism triggers, and we attempt to determine every single step of the way;

how it comes, when, how the package looks and where to pick it up. This approach does not work.

That's not commitment, that's control.

If we wait until we are ready we might never be.

Many times we reject situations coming to our life because:

a. We believe we are not ready.

b. We believe we are not worthy.

c. We believe we need to have everything perfectly aligned to welcome that new thing.

d. We are slow.

What if life only brought to you events, people and experiences that you are ready for, and that you actually need to reach the next level?

What if every single thing that appears in front of you is somehow created and asked for by you?

Would that make a difference in the way you approach life?

Would this help you stop controlling every single thing that comes to you?

Sometimes, the thing we want to commit to the most comes when we least expect it. What are you going to do, reject it because it doesn't come according to your agenda, and you have a hair appointment next Thursday?

Let's say the job of your life appears, and you are like, *"Not now, I need to buy a pair of shoes first!"* Sounds funny, but we pull this type of shit all the time.

I have a really funny example for this one:

Somehow, every time I started a relationship, I would attract some sort of magical guru reading to tell me if the new guy was "the One" or not. And guess what happened? I ate the whole thing up, time and time again. I was so reliant on those so-called visions, feeling like a victim of fate and completely ignoring the fact that my actions and his actions were what actually defined the future of the relationship.

These readings were right sometimes, and they were wrong sometimes. In my last relationship, with Gardenia Guy, there was a girl that told me he was "the One." Finally, someone telling me that I was actually on the right track. What a relief! Turns out he wasn't, or we weren't, or we were, but we weren't both fully committed.

The point is, I half-assed my inner knowingness by always being influenced by that specific message from the universe.

So, when the guru person would tell me "Yes," I would try, with all my power, to control the unfolding of the relationship, and when the guru person would say "No," I would have a back door wide open and allow doubt to creep in, because a whiny voice in my head would say: *"What if she was right?"*

It's weird, I know, and definitely embarrassing to share this with you, but it's the truth. I could completely ignore all other signs from the universe if a person called a "medium" or a "psychic" gave me their view on something, sometimes without me even asking!

And the funniest thing is, I worked for several years as a tarot reader! Every client I had, I would tell them:

"This is not a reading to tell you a future written in stone. Your future can change depending on where you are standing right now. So, if you are looking for a type of reading that will tell a future, and you will just believe it, this is not the place. I am here to help you access your present and see what it is you actually want. If you change, your future will change as well."

Somehow, I never heard myself, and this annoying cosmic joke kept biting me in the ass.

"Unless it comes out of
your soul like a rocket,
unless being still would
drive you to madness or
suicide or murder,
don't do it.

Unless the sun inside you
is burning your gut,
don't do it.

When it is truly time,
and if you have been chosen,
it will do it by itself and it
will keep on doing it until
you die or it dies in you.

There is no other way.
And there never was."

Charles Bukowski

Chapter 5

PASSION

The fire under your ass[1]

> "She is mad but she is magic,
> there is no lie in her fire."
>
> Bukowski

Fire. Energy. Intensity. Zest. Enthusiasm. Shine. Desire. Thrill. Excitement. Intensity. Vibrancy. Eagerness. Outburst. Vehemence.

I might sound illiterate, but I was in absolute shock when I researched, just now, the origin of the word *passion*. It comes from the Latin *pati*, which means *"to suffer."*

To suffer?! What an odd evolution! From suffering to, as nowadays used in a colloquial style, experiencing intense emotion towards something or someone.

---

[1] Note from the Author: I am aware that this chapter is the only one titled with a word that does not begin with a "C". I don't really care. Passion cannot be called anything else. However, if you really do care and it makes your word-OCD squirm, you can refer to this chapter as "Cookies".

I suppose that when you are passionate about something, you are willing to walk through hellfire in order to obtain that which you are passionate about. Maybe that's where the whole suffering thing comes from. It's my guess anyway, as I really don't know.

It only takes watching a few Mexican soap operas, *telenovelas,* to see how passion is viewed sometimes. There you'll get people slapping people, people killing people, and people inventing lies and stories about people, just to get to the person or thing they are passionate about. They are more passionate about what they hate than what they love. Often the villains are the ones with the passion, and the "good" characters are all about love and crying. Passion does whatever it takes, even if it means war, while love just sits and suffers, and wins because it's pretty.

What a bunch of crap! It's funny to have those two forces working in opposing fields, with one feeding off the other.

Love is a state of being; passion is the amount of love running through our veins.

On second thought, don't watch any soaps. It's a waste of time, and in my case, it took a lot of meditation to remove many childhood impressions of what a passionate person looks like, and how it's not cool to slap a guy.

Anyhow, I am much more interested in talking about *passion* now.

Passion moves the world. Passion keeps you going when you have no other motivation. Passion is the element that enables commitment to keep going once the initial *oomph* has faded.

Passion is the fuel of life.

The Sun is the passion of this Earth. It´s what makes things grow, what nurtures and what provides shine and life to everything. Without the Sun, we would all wither. Withering is no fun.

Passion is the life force that flows through our veins, so, unless you are a zombie in disguise, you have passion. Trust me, you do.

If I could have added to the cover of this book:

"Bonus: 200 pounds of free passion!" I would have.

I would give away passion to every single human on Earth, because I believe that a passionate person can create wonders in this world.

I am an extremely intense person. I feel every single thing running through me, every tiny thing around me. I feel people´s thoughts, people´s energies, and I feel every single impact my own thoughts have in my body. I feel music as if they were feelings.

In the words of Donna Summer, *"I feel love..."* and everything else, I will add.

I love that about me now, but I used to resist being this intense so much. I can feel passion even if I don´t have anything to be passionate about.

Throughout my life, that passion was directed many times towards destruction and self-sabotage. What do you do when you have all this fire burning inside, but no idea what to do with it? How do you give it away without scorching yourself, and others, in the process? How do you direct passion towards greatness? That has been one of my biggest quests in life.

You don't have to be like me, passionate about absolutely everything. Believe me, I've heard more than once that I have a bit too much fire in my heart. I sometimes feel passion when I go to the convenience store and I see a cold Coca-Cola, so yes, my passion is and has been very intense. It comes with its perks and with its curses, and it's taken me many, many years to learn to direct all that passion for the good.

I just felt like a superhero right there, using my powers for good.

However, when it comes to choosing between passion and not passion, I choose the first. Always.

When we are passionate, our ass moves. And we need more people moving their ass to be able to rock this world into a different reality.

EVERYONE'S HEART SINGS FOR SOMETHING

Not everyone is passionate in their expression. You only need to take samples from different countries to see that.

Latinos show more passion: in our food, in our music, in the chaotic traffic, in our hundreds of parties, in our loudness, in our hugs, in the excess use of emoticons in our text messages.

Nordics show less passion: in their food, in their music, in their organized traffic, in their social gatherings, in their leveled voices, in their handshakes, in their properly written text messages.

The reason behind it is not up to me to explain or attempt to discuss, since I am no expert in genetics or social anthropology. But I've spent a good amount of time with people from many different countries, and I've seen that these differences are in fact palpable.

At the six-month meditation retreat I did in Spain, there were, like, 70 people from many different countries: Mexico, Norway, UK, New Zealand, Australia, US, Canada, Spain, Venezuela and Holland. For the first three months, we had, like, 35 Mexicans on the course, but in the last three months, the Mexicans had to leave and continue the course back home because of visa regulations. I got to stay because I had a student visa, along with another four Mexicans.

The morning after all the Mexicans had left, I arrived at breakfast at 8 in the morning, and it felt like I was arriving at someone's funeral. It was so quiet. I looked around, trying to figure out what had changed, what was different that morning. I couldn't quite put my finger on it, and then suddenly I got it. It was the absence of Latinos! No one singing, no one hugging, no one exuding joy at such an early time in the morning.

It was a big problem, so we had to come up with a creative solution. We created the "Mexican for a Week" program. What did it entail? People from other countries would volunteer to become Mexican for a week. They would get a Mexican name and be given different tasks, like hugging everyone, being loud at dining times, sharing with an excess of love in the meditation meetings and dancing while they did the dishes.

One day, during a meeting, one of my classmates from England, Dharma Raj, or should I say José Juan Sandoval de la Alta, from Monterrey, stood up and shared how this Mexican program had transformed him:

"It's as if I was given permission to be loving, to be expressive, to be joyful. I grew up in a very cold country, where all these attitudes are outside the rules of etiquette. This has been very liberating."

Of course, all the true Mexicans, as well as the Mexicans for a week, stood up and clapped and cheered.

So, regardless of whether your outer expression is passionate or not, regardless where you are from or how your upbringing was, you do have a heart and it does work – I hope.

Having been given a heart, you were also given a flame that lives within it.

And that flame sings whenever something resonates with it. However, when the flame isn't on, that means there is a gas leak, and we all know what happens then: we become sleepy, toxic and it stinks.

We all came with a certain set of experiences that will naturally fuel that fire. You don't choose what does or doesn't ignite you, it just naturally happens that way. That is the reason why there are so many people doing so many different things in this world.

What were you passionate about when you were a child? Do you remember?

Raindrops racing down the window! I remember that I loved watching the raindrops race down the car window when we were traveling. Sometimes, two drops would meet up, reunite and create a bigger drop. It made me feel so joyful inside.

Talk, talk, talk! I was so passionate about talking that I spoke faster than my mind could run. According to my father, I spoke before I started walking.

Singing, dancing, reading, and writing. I would talk to my mom about my day while practicing dance steps that I learned at ballet class. I wrote my first poem when I was five, and I started reading when I was four. I had to listen to my mom yell at me every night to stop reading, turn the light off and go to sleep.

I was so passionate about stories. When I was in kindergarten, I learned the whole script of the Christmas play, and I would repeat it all, doing all the different characters, and I would tape myself doing it with a little cassette recorder. I remember I was so sad when I wasn't chosen to act in the play – I only got to be a singing elf – but my passion for creating didn't stop me from doing it at home. And when there were no school plays, I would use my Barbies to create a whole world.

Dad´s home! I was passionate about my dad coming home every afternoon. I would run through the hall as soon as I heard the door, and he would crouch down with arms wide open to hug me. I´ll tell you, this specific passion gave me a few bruises on my knees from the many times I fell and slide across the floor.

Cooking. Even though I could not reach the cupboards, I was passionate about recipes and baking cakes or making breakfast. My poor parents! I wonder how many things they had to eat after a night of partying. That´s love right there.

Five more minutes! There was no passion like waking up for school, running to my parents' room and jump into their bed to be hugged by my dad for five more minutes. He would scratch my back and I would sleep again. Five more minutes always turned into 25 more minutes, and a kid arriving late for school.

I was really passionate about sharing with my friends, laughing with them, creating choreographies or games or plays, and hanging out in our own little world for hours. My mom started allowing me to go to their houses more often after the phone bill arrived and she discovered that when I wasn´t with my friends, I was spending hours on the phone with them!

Pedro Infante's black and white films! Every Saturday at 2pm, I would be sitting in front of the TV, and nothing could distract me from that.

All of these things made me feel truly myself; made me feel beautiful, made me feel shining. I was a little shining body when I was doing or experiencing these things.

**True passions make you feel
like you are a shining light.**

Have my passions changed? Not much. I am still passionate about creating new worlds, about hanging out with my friends in our own little world, about classic films, about singing, dancing, reading and writing. I am still passionate about that hug I get to give my dad whenever I see him.

I am still passionate about hanging out with my best friend, Ishani, in our own crazy, funky world that no one else understands, where we speak our own made-up language. I am passionate about talking to her for hours, and sending her 10-minute audio messages when we are apart.

I am passionate now about getting to know new people and places, and bringing goods back to my friends and loved ones.

Five more minutes became having a passion for holding my boyfriend's hand while being held by him in the mornings. It brings me passion to see how his eyes sparkle when he talks about something he is passionate about.

I am still passionate about cooking and making big meals for the people I love. There is just something about it. Maybe they, too, like my parents, are forced to eat something disgusting. If that's the case, I hope I never get to find out.

Passion comes easy to someone who recognizes that the choice of freedom is an easy one to make. Whether it's *Game of Thrones* and *Friends*, or teaching meditation all over the world, I am extremely passionate about my interests, and love sharing my approach to experiencing consciousness with whoever wants to live this life fully.

HANDS ON ASS 4: THE PASSION

What were your passions then, and what are your passions now? Write them down, don't be lazy. You will have a lot of fun. Notice how, when you are doing it, your heart fills with warmth. That is your fire lighting up!

GIVE ME PASSION AND I WILL GIVE YOU THE WORLD

Passion is not the opposite of calm.

That would be the same as saying that focus is the opposite of patience.

I love hearing someone talking with passion about what they love. They can be the calmest, most low- voiced person, and yet still transmit all the passion their heart is carrying towards their topic of interest.

One of my monk friends, Garuda, is an English guy that you would not define as passionate. He is serene, his voice is low and smooth, and his movements are fine and delicate. But when he talks about consciousness, Sanskrit or Vedic traditions, he has the power to make you feel the vibrancy of his heart. The same thing happens when he speaks about his wife or his children. You zone into his world and experience every single thing he is saying. That is passion.

It does not look any certain way, this passion thing. We are all passionate about something, and there are as many passions as there are people on this planet. How amazing that is! Imagine everyone being passionate about painting. We would have a world without accountants, and what a nightmare that would be! A world without cooks? No way!

I praise everyone and their personal passions, because they make this world the wonderful kaleidoscope of expression that it is.

Sadly, though, not many people follow their passion. Many don't even know what they are passionate about, or what is to truly feel passionate!

When you are flowing in what makes you feel passionate, you are resting in what gives you life, and that's a major hint for living whole-ass: engaging in those aspects that make you feel on fire.

Your passion resides in your strengths; in your unique character traits that you and only you carry. These are natural to you, and they give you a full spectrum of applications for your passion.

Focusing on our strengths and other people's strengths can uplift your reality and change it for the better.

Yes, it's cool to see our limitations and overcome our weaknesses, but passion is all about uplifting and celebrating our power, and embracing our differences.

Recently, I was asked to do an exercise which involved describing my unique strengths and abilities, i.e. my superpowers. Not pretend superpowers, like flying – even though I believe it will one day be possible – but real ones.

HANDS ON ASS 5: THE SUPERPOWERS

Write down the names of five people you admire. It can be people in your life or famous people, dead or alive, it doesn't make a difference.

Write down why you admire them. If you feel like writing down more people, do it.

This is my list:

1. **My Dad.** Creative, funny and joyful, enthusiast, loving, talented, always trying new things, always finds a way to do what he desires, giving, generous, has a different view on things, wise, patient, fearless, always looking for different ways to serve, passionate about life, always takes care of his family, looks out for others.

2. **My Teacher.** Ability to connect with everyone, funny, fearless, light, extremely wise, inspiring, patient, free, generous, direct, adventurous, passionate about life and consciousness, always offers a different way of seeing things, joyful, has great taste, can communicate the truth in many different ways, loves unconditionally, never compromises the Truth.

3. **John Lennon.** Sought truth, talented, unique, creative, passionate about peace, direct, sense of humor, great performer, used his fame for expanding good,

communicated the truth, didn't care what others thought, intense.

4. Ishani, my best friend. Extremely loving, has a unique view on people and things, truthful, doesn't have filters, creative, really funny, lives in her own magical world, so joyful, goes for what she wants, free, believes in people, light, intense, passionate.

5. Einstein. Wise, different view on things, eloquent writer, romantic, passionate, knew there was something beyond intellect, sense of humor.

6. Tha Menon, my cousin. Fearless, always looking to be better, relaxed about life, doesn't care what people think, free, follows his heart, funny, lives with passion, light, naturally wise, always makes his environment relaxed and lighter.

I quickly discovered that I could've picked 50 more people, but I am not going to bore you with a longest list. If you feel inspired to do carry on, do not stop. It brought a lot of joy to my heart as I listed every person and focused on their strengths.

If you want to take it one step further, send an email to everyone on your list, letting them know why you admire them. It will be tricky with the likes of Einstein and Lennon, but worth a try!

> Now, circle out the qualities those people have in common.

My list:

- Funny

- Loving

- Passionate

- Truth

- Different view of the world

- Joyful

- Creative/ Talented

- Finding ways to give/ generous

- Wisdom

- Fearless

- Light

For me, lightness is something I've always admired. I tend to be very light when I am at my best, whereas when I am in my "dark side," lightness is not something that I can just grab and wear. So, that is a strength I want to have, and is one that I've been developing throughout the years.

Connect the dots:

The traits you admire most are either the strengths you have or the strengths you would like to have.

It's not so difficult to know which ones are which.

> Recognize your strengths and own them. Sit with them. It's virtually impossible to see something in others if you don't have the same potential in yourself, too. You admire them for a reason; you feel that attraction for a reason.
>
> Now you know which are your strengths, and which are the traits you would like to develop.

There is a really cool movement called Let it Ripple. They make films that encourage change. You can check out on YouTube their video *The Science of Character*, which might give you a broader view on character traits and developing our strengths.

There is no time to belittle ourselves or to focus solely on our weaknesses. That is so old. Humbleness is not the absence of love and praise for your wonderful self. Humbleness is recognizing that we were given our strengths for a reason, and so we need to use them in service to this world and to others. Arrogant would be keeping all these gifts locked inside, where they can't be used for good.

HANDS ON ASS 6: EXPLOIT THE SUPERPOWERS

List your superpowers, your abilities and your talents. You already have some hints. Now make them unique. What makes YOU unique? Sit with this. If you really do not have a clue, talk to your friends, to your family or to whoever it is that you trust, and look for common threads.

My superpowers:

- Clarity, bravery and dedication to truth

- Witty sense of humor, joyful

- I can allow people to be themselves and be OK with who they are

- Creative mind, seeing life through different eyes.

- I can teach people how to have fun

- Communication and sharing of complex concepts with a down to earth, digestible and light language.

- I spot bullshit when other people talk. I can tell the underlying truth of their hearts.

- People reader

- Extremely loving and giving, able to connect with people from different backgrounds.

- I tear down concepts and comfort zones.

- I connect great people with other great people.

You might find is not so easy to acknowledge some of your strengths. You will see patterns and resistances come up. That's why it's so cool to share this with the people that love you.

'Loving? Me? Nah.'

I heard that in my mind many times when doing this exercise, as my friends kept telling me how extremely loving I was. Every time I heard it, I cringed. My head would go, like, *"No, fuckin' way, I am not loving. I love, but loving? Me?"*

Turns out, I heard it so many times that I ended up recognizing the truth! And once I embraced it, the loving aspect of me started shining through, with no effort or *"working on myself"* required.

This exercise takes courage, so take as much time as you need. Remember, this is not the time to be tiny – go as big as you can. You are describing a superhero. Your strengths need to be something that will allow you to be the full expression of your inner superhero; to be whole-ass.

Good, well done. Now you have your set of strengths and abilities. This will help you spark-up your passion for life, and you'll start to do what you are meant to be doing!

> Pick every strength you have and write down three different ways you can apply them. You might notice some of them are seldom used!

My list:

- Clarity, bravery and dedication to truth

  - ✓ Writing about truth
  - ✓ Teaching meditation
  - ✓ Speaking my truth

- Witty sense of humor, joyful

  - ✓ Hang out with people who I can laugh with
  - ✓ Write blogs
  - ✓ Read and watch things that make me laugh

- I can allow people to be themselves and be OK with who they are.

  - ✓ Praise people more
  - ✓ Motivate people.
  - ✓ Be more myself

- Creative mind, seeing life through different eyes.

  - ✓ Write more from my point of view
  - ✓ Treat everything I do as art
  - ✓ Use my hands more

- I can teach people how to have fun.

  ✓ Attend more social events
  ✓ Teach more about lightness of being
  ✓ Share the joy!

- Communication and sharing of complex concepts with down to earth, digestible and light language.

  ✓ Write more blogs!
  ✓ Teach more courses
  ✓ Do podcasts

- I spot bullshit when other people talk. I can tell the underlining truth in their hearts.

  ✓ Be willing to speak my truth
  ✓ Open the space for people to be honest
  ✓ Do more readings

- People reader

  ✓ Apply the same as the previous point

- Extremely loving and giving, able to connect with people from different backgrounds.

  ✓ Express my love even more
  ✓ Reach out more to people
  ✓ Write a thank you note to everyone I love.

- I tear down concepts and comfort zones.

  ✓ Don´t hold back on being who I am

- ✓ Write more about this
- ✓ Be an example

- I connect great people with other great people.

  - ✓ Travel more to connect people
  - ✓ Create a network
  - ✓ Talk more to my friends about my other friends

The steps to take can be either practical or internal, it doesn't matter. What matters is that you take them and that you fuel your own passion by being that which makes you feel powerful.

"Just take the best from the people around you... and you'll always be better!"

Tha Menon

PASSION IS AN ATTITUDE

You are a superhero. Have you ever seen a superhero who is not passionate about their mission? No, not even dark Batman. So, you'd better start behaving like the superhero you are, and quit hiding behind the tux, or the glasses, if your preference is Superman.

Do you have to wait until you feel passion to engage life? No. If you are feeling flat, pick one of the many things that you now know will ignite your passion and start doing it. I don't care if at first you feel like a corpse while baking cookies, just do it. In no time, you'll feel life flowing through your veins again.

Dare to sing, to dance and to get wet under the rain. Dare to be a more colorful version of yourself. Don't be in awe, provoke the awe! That's why the word *awe-some* was invented!

About two years ago, the relationship with Gardenia Guy ended. I was absolutely devastated. My cookie had crumbled, and I had no idea what to do with myself, with my life or with all the feelings of despair.

I had been living at the beach with him, and I didn't even know if I should move cities – again! – or not. All I knew was that I had wonderful techniques to get me through, and that I was definitely going to get through it. I just didn't know when.

I had an upcoming meditation course, and that morning I had to go and teach a free introductory talk to a bunch of people interested in Ascension. I was sitting at a

Starbucks, coffee in hand, with what seemed to be bee stings for eyes, crying.

"How the hell am I going to share with these people about peace, joy and love if I feel like this? I am no one to share! I am a failure!"

I couldn't ask someone to stand in for me, as there were no other teachers in town, and it was too late to cancel. I texted my Teacher:

Stupid mornings. It's difficult for me to accept reality as it is. I am so angry right now and I want to yell at him for leaving me alone. Stupid, stupid boy. I have an intro talk in 20 minutes and I am crying my balls out at a Starbucks like a sissy.

> *You can't be crying your balls out because you have no balls. You are a girl.*

Maybe I am crying his baby balls out.

As you can see, I was very, very angry, and deep in my emotions.

> *Make the intro talk about them, and not you. It will help. It is very important for you that you make your day about God, and not about you.*

More complaining on my side... then:

Ok! I'll do that! I'll watch your videos again, you always make me smile.

> *Smiling is always good.*

I'll tape myself some smiles.

> *They say if you put a smile on your face all day, it is impossible to feel sad or depressed.*

Will fake smile and see if it catches up.

> *Apparently it does...*

Like this?

Insert here a picture of me, with the fakest smile, and the reddest face ever.

> *That's perfect.*

The press is here and I am wearing no makeup!

> *That is making it about YOU.*

Touché.

I walked in and did the talk, and eight people signed up for the course. Somehow, in the middle of it all, I shared from a place of peace what I was going through. Later that weekend, during the course, two people told me that what inspired them to come to sign up was seeing how gracefully I was going through a tough time, without trying to mask it with a "spiritual" face. They told me that they wanted to experience that realness, and being present with what was up.

And I was passionate all the way through my talk.

**So, when you feel no passion, no smile, fake it!
Fake it till you feel it. It's all an attitude.**

"Passion directed
towards absolute truth
heals this world."

Maharishi Krishnananda Ishaya

PASSION TRAP

Let's say you are one of those people, like me, who are naturally intense and passionate.

If your passion doesn't have a direction – a proper one – or a purpose, it can become a self-destructive force which leads to a shitload of drama. Those are the main traps when it comes to passion.

Why? Because all that energy needs an outlet. It's there for a reason, and it needs to be given form in this world. You were born with that excess because you have the ability to use it. It's already there, so fighting it or trying to get rid of it is futile. Believe me, I tried for years.

Addictions, habits, emotional explosions, self-violence, external violence, drama, tears, anger; you name it, I've been there. All those are by-products of a passion that is not being properly harnessed.

I used to tend to have very extreme periods of intense energy bottled up in my body. I would feel like a bomb had exploded inside me; I was on fire, and I couldn't find a big enough hose in the world to put myself out. Add to that an awful feeling of disgust towards myself. I hated it, I hated myself for being like this, but couldn't seem to remove it. I wished I was different, I wished I was more like my friends: calmer, more serene and less *me*.

Drinking, smoking weed and having sex were all used to shake this off. Drinking would help me get rid of the excess all right, but it would usually bring with it more drama, chaos, or actions that I would regret later, especially the morning after.

Weed, well, it would remove the edge, that's for sure, but the next morning it would be there again, and ironically, the monster that lived inside me would apparently feed off of it. Sex? Well, yes, a great outlet where passion would explode everywhere, only to end unsatisfied because either the guy had no idea what he was doing, or because ultimately the sharing of souls wasn't really there, and that was what I always craved.

In the words of Natalie Imbruglia, I was torn. I would crank up the songs that would make me feel the emotions even more, to see if that would get rid of it, but if anything, it would amp it up! I would end up madder, sadder and higher on the scale of intensity.

To be honest, sometimes, like this morning when it came up, the old disgust comes back. I did find it extremely funny and useful, knowing that I was dedicating my morning to writing about it, but thank God that it only lasts an hour tops now.

If I had a boyfriend, the object of my passion had a direction - a totally misdirected one. I would indulge completely in that passion, making it all about them. They had to satisfy that passion, physically, emotionally, mentally and spiritually. And when that wasn't met, guess what? More self-destruction would follow.

"But I am passionate, so what can I do about it? This is who I am, I can't change it. Even though I hate it, you better be OK with me being a basket case!"

It would become a never-ending loop of emotion that ultimately destroyed me. I could definitely not love that aspect of myself.

Feeding it didn't work, trying to get rid of it didn't work, numbing it didn't work and directing it towards someone else didn't work. What a pickle.

Catharsis came when my boyfriend broke up with me over the phone when I was 20 years old. I spent four hours crying, sitting in the bathtub at my mother's house – you gotta make the scene dramatic, that's what artists do! – feeling absolutely broken. The direction I had given my passion to for the last year was suddenly removed, and I felt as if I had literally imploded and died.

Lying in my mother's bed, I suddenly unplugged. I closed my eyes, and there was nothing: no thought, no feeling, no sense of self. The most peaceful nothingness I've ever hanged out in, where everything was perfect; where there was no "me" to be perfected, or to have to deal with emotions or breakups. It was an ocean of heaven, and it lasted for a couple of hours.

Destruction resumed when I became aware of what was happening. I didn't eat or sleep for seven days. I would call him every morning to beg him to take me back. This feeling was eating me up, and I thought that only he had the power to alleviate the suffering.

"I think I am dying soon. I can't bear this. This cannot be life. If life means coming here, suffering like a motherfucker, surviving and dying, then I don't want it. There has to be something better than this."

I was telling this to my friend Mariana, while she was attempting to give me a massage, and she said she couldn't even touch me without feeling dense.

"Well, there is something better than this."

My eyes opened up in disbelief. What the hell was she talking about? Everyone seems to be suffering through life. *"Oh, really?"*

"Yes, REALLY. Do you want to give it a try?"

"At this point, I'll try rubbing an egg over my body while dancing naked if it means getting rid of this."

She gave me a phone number, and I called a woman that told me I needed to make space for an hour, for four days in a row. She showed up at my house that same afternoon.

She got me to lay down on my bed and started doing weird things. My head wouldn't stop going and going, the emotion stuck everywhere. *"When is she going to finish? What on Earth is she doing?"* Boom! World stops again. An intense sense of peace and well-being invaded me, my room and the Earth. I felt as if my whole brain was rewired.

When she finished, she told me:

"You need to remember, the truth is inside. True love is inside. You are here to wake up."

Holy fuck! I'd been looking in the wrong direction all that time! It seemed like I always knew this, but that I had only just remembered. It was as silly as suddenly remembering where you misplaced your keys.

Anthony de Mello. That name came to me, as I saw the image of a book I had seen in my mother's library. I ran towards it and opened it:

Happiness is you.

Dude, I tell you, it was like once I remembered where truth and love actually lived, a series of magical events unfolded for me. A road that was always there in front of me, waving at me, yelling, pointing, suddenly came into focus.

All that misplaced passion found its proper direction, and the following years were about finding the right path; the path that would actually lead me to Self-Realization. So, if you ask me, the best way to place your passion is towards self-awareness. From there, everything becomes a passion, every moment is awe-inspiring, and your real, passionate self begins to shine through.

"Courage is grace
under pressure."

Ernest Hemingway

Chapter 6

COURAGE

The not giving a monkey's ass

Knights, conquerors, adventurers, travelers to unknown lands and people surviving natural catastrophes. They all share something in common: courage. However, it's not only great acts of human power that reveal courage. Courage is found every day in the tiniest of actions, in the most hidden moments.

We all have the power to be everyday heroes.

There is no limit to courage. Stepping through the known into the unknown always takes courage. Stepping through your limiting thoughts, your habitual reactions, your comfort zones, what frightens you, speaking up, defending yourself... Growth resides on the other side of every courageous moment.

> "You know, sometimes all you need is twenty seconds of insane courage. Just literally twenty seconds of just embarrassing bravery. And I promise you, something great will come of it."
>
> Benjamin Mee (Matt Damon)
> We Bought a Zoo (2011)

There is no whole-assing without growth. That would be the same as eating fries without ketchup – what's the point, really? A whole-ass person grows constantly, and does whatever it takes to finish the day greater and freer than the when they woke up that morning.

Courage is the ultimate element. You might have the ingredients, but without the oven, there'll be no cheesecake. Commitment, clarity and passion are the elements; courage is the motion that enables you to engage yourself, your life and this world with all you've got, and to make the best out of your every passing moment.

Boldness and the willingness to be silly are a great combination. They can create the biggest of fuck-ups, but they can also make the most amazing dreams tangible.

We live in such fear of fucking up. I know I do. Always waiting for the recrimination, for the judging finger, for receiving a message from any part of the universe telling me: "*Oh, dude, you went too far. You totally fucked up!*"

What a limited way to live! How many dreams we leave as just an idea, simply because we are not bold or brave enough to go with it and explore where the road ends?

Even if it's a dead-end street with a toxic waste exit, ultimately, who freaking cares? Do you think you are going to be on your deathbed thinking of all the things you did that didn't go right? No. What eats us up are the things we don't do or say, because we're scared of what *might* happen.

You will never know if you don't dare to act.

A lot of us were raised to aim for perfection, or at least our idea of *perfect*. Many of us are raised to believe that things only matter if others recognize them as excellent. Otherwise, no cookie for us.

As a child, I was a model student, one of these wizard kids that did everything well, from math to grammar to art. I could stand up in front of hundreds of people and give a speech, and get a standing ovation. I didn't try to do it, it just came easily to me. Everywhere I went, I just heard praise for how adorable and what perfect a genius I was.

As I grew up and the hormones hit me, I moved far away from that. I was distracted, reckless, emotional and couldn't care less about doing anything right. I did care about my parents' approval, though, just as I cared about being accepted by my social group, which rarely happened since I was never one to follow the rules. All I heard was how I was not going to achieve anything in life, and that I was throwing it all away.

The subsequent feelings of disappointment at not getting credit unless I did things right ended up biting me in the ass on many occasions. Hell, I'm writing this chapter after a six-month siesta from putting words to page, which I am sure has a lot to do with the unconscious expectation that I might end up hearing:

"You fucked up. Bad, bad human!"

> "Do not be too timid and squeamish about your actions. All life is an experiment. The more experiments you make the better. What if they are a little coarse and you may get your coat soiled or torn? What if you do fail, and get fairly rolled in the dirt once or twice? Up again, you shall never be so afraid of a tumble."
>
> Ralph Waldo Emerson

And you know what, who cares? Who cares even if you do get the big red X. Is that going to make you less human? No. Does that take away points from your scoreboard, and therefore you will die sooner? No. Does it take away all the experience you could have gained from the journey of whatever endeavor you were on? No.

Seeking approval stands in the way of courage.

HANDS ON ASS 7: THE APPROVAL SEARCH

Write down all the things you have stopped yourself from doing/saying/asking/being because you were stopped by the approval need.

Timeline? A week. Just this past week.

The exercise is not designed so that you can give yourself your own sign of disapproval, but so you become aware of certain patterns.

Some of us seek approval in our intimate relationships. I know that's my Achilles heel. I care so much what my partner, my dad and my spiritual teacher all think of what I do or how I behave. It's not their fault or their responsibility, but secretly I wished they would always tell me: *"You are doing great, keep going."* Whenever I have to do something and their opinion is involved, I feel a rush of scary energy in my body before I receive a response. Nine out of ten times, the response is great, but I know what my mind is expecting in those seconds it takes to open the email or read the message: *"You suck, you did it wrong – again!"*

Waiting for fatal feedback.

For others, the search for approval is in their social circles; the expanded circles of acquaintances, friends and colleagues. They are paralyzed, and waste lots of energy attempting to gain approval from the people they surround themselves with. So, attempting to dress in a different way? No way. Attempting to change course in life and dedicate myself to something unorthodox? No way. Daring to speak up when I see something off? No way. Courage freezes, and we hide ourselves in a corner.

And now we have the wonderful, super real world of social media. A lot of people are constantly seeking approval there, applying more credit to how many likes they got that day than to their children making them a drawing. Attempting to be approved by an invisible entity, which is truly so fickle when it comes to giving out "Likes," is courage suicide.

So, approval and the need for acceptance are the venoms that kill boldness and the willingness to be seen as silly – the willingness to fuck up! It´s so liberating to realize it.

Teenagers are a great example of this. Sure, they might go over the top sometimes and really screw up, but part of the experience in those years is about testing boundaries, doing new stuff and feeling the rush of being bold, whether it is through skipping class or dancing silly in the middle of a supermarket.

HANDS ON ASS 8: THE BOLD ONE

You guessed it! Be bold. Be you. Dare to be seen as silly, dare to say what comes, dare to explore a different road and dare to ask for what you want.

Dare to dream, and most importantly, dare to go after it. Whatever the result, you won´t regret it. You will reach the other side a completely different person.

REALITY IS IN YOUR FACE. FACE IT.

I assume, even though I shouldn´t, that everyone is acquainted with the expression "Shit happens." Shit does happen. Life happens. Circumstances happen. Quite often, those circumstances do not meet our expectations, our desires or our ideals.

Sometimes, really tough shit happens.

The question is not whether it happens or not, because it will. The question is, what are you going to do about it? How are you going to respond when shit happens? Are you going to face it, fight it or flee from it?

The worst thing I've ever had to face was my mom falling into a kind of coma, when all her toxins went up to her brain because her liver wasn't doing its job due to Cirrhosis.

It was a random morning, and her husband called me and told me I should come home. My mom had been in treatment for a while and she wasn't in good shape, but this time she was in the hospital, completely disconnected from reality.

All the blood rushed to my legs, and I heard myself saying: *"I'll try to organize everything so I can maybe be there in a week."* Yes, I was being a complete wimp, not wanting to face reality at all. What you can't see won't hurt you, right? Luckily, he was direct with me:

"No, now. You have got to come now."

And I did. And when I arrived later that day, reality slapped me in the face. She was not there at all. She was not my amazing, strong, beautiful mother. She was a sick person that couldn't so much as control her bowel movements, and she did not even know who I was. She stayed like that for two weeks or so, and suddenly my reality was a different one. I was living in a hospital, watching her babble incoherently and getting excited about any little sign of recognition. She looked like a yellow balloon.

It took so much courage not to run away, or to try and mask reality and pretend like everything was going to be OK. The biggest fear of my life was confronting me: losing one of the two amazing beings that gave me life.

I had the biggest angels around me, to keep me in touch with reality and not let me face the other way or hide behind any stupid reaction. I had to be there fully for her, and love her with all I had.

She came back to this reality, and eventually we left the hospital. She moved to Monterrey, the city where I used to live, to wait for a liver transplant. There was not a moment when I wasn't worried or aware of her. I spent all my days with her. I was tired, scared and confused, but there wasn't time to indulge in that, because what she needed was love, motivation and joy. I did my best to give her exactly that.

Every so often, we had to run to the hospital because her brain was intoxicated again. I never knew when or if she would come back. It was constant exhaustion and constant worry, yet somehow, there was so much joy and peace, and I couldn't count the many amazing moments, full of love, that I lived through those months. Humans have the amazing ability to adapt to any circumstance.

A 32-year-old baby being constantly faced with living without her mother was a constant invitation to step through. Otherwise, I'd have been eaten up. You can always go to your inner dark corner and hide underneath your safety blanket until the storm passes, but thank God I did not do that, because this time, when the storm finally passed, it carried my mother away.

Courage didn't stop at the hospital bill. It had to keep going when faced with the scariest reality of them all: she was gone. Courage needs to keep going when you are attending the funeral, when you are clearing out her clothes, when you are cooking one month later and you call her to ask about the recipe, only to remember that her phone has been disconnected. Courage needs to keep going even three years later, writing these lines and accepting again that it happened.

Reality is as it is, and being courageous enables us to face it with open arms and heart, without hiding from or fighting it. Grace presents itself and reveals that even in the most horrible times in life, there is love, peace and perfection.

Face reality, whatever it is. It is already happening and it is going to happen with or without you.

THE DEVIL HIDES IN THE DETAILS

In the last couple of days, I've hit a serious bump with my partner. Clashing heads like rams, I went so deep down the rabbit hole that I had no idea if the relationship was even going to survive. My whole body felt uncomfortable, constrained and painful. I needed to get out of it, but I had no idea how to do it.

I kept trying to pretend everything was OK within me, and kept trying to put some sugar on top of the shit. My warrior persona kept thinking that the most courageous thing to do was to grab my shit and go do whatever it takes for me not to feel this icky, yucky despair. It's funny when these things happen, because even the house looked darker, and where there used to be laughter, now there was growling.

So yes, I could've just left, and the pain probably would've gone away. But how much would it have served me? Not much.

Here's why:

It took even more courage to stick around and accept the fact that there was an issue to be addressed. Leaving is easy. It took balls to sit with it and let life start showing me the way out, instead of trying to figure it out myself.

It took courage to talk; to speak up, open myself in front of him and reveal my truth. It took courage to stand up for my truth, even if it meant losing him. It took courage to leave for a friend's house, not really knowing if this was the end or not.

What I got in return was courage. It took courage on his side to come to my friend's house and talk about the situation in front of other people. It took courage to expose his feelings and be vulnerable. As Ishayas, we always ask for help from others when we can't solve things ourselves, but when it is something so personal, it takes courage to go on and actually do it.

It took courage from both of us to leave that place together, still unsure if we were going to make it through. And it takes courage to stay committed to the relationship, even when we are uncertain. It takes courage to accept that life has a plan of its own, well outside of our control. Our best shot is to keep giving 100% all the time, however bleak it looks at any given moment.

Now we are sitting beside each other, writing in the garden, under a lucky sunny day in England. It takes courage to be willing to let the past go and approach the relationship with brand new eyes. Even if it's uncertain, even if you don't know if the other person will leave, or even if you have no idea what is coming around the corner. It takes courage to say, *"I love you."*

It's the little details that create character.

It is facing our daily attitudes, our everyday issues and our relationship dynamics that takes courage. It is willing to be who you weren't and letting what you thought you were dissolve, so that a new version of you can arise. It is being open to stepping into vulnerable waters, even if you are not certain that you will arrive at a safe shore. It is putting yourself out there, constantly on the line, exposing your truth with all of your being, regardless of what comes back. It takes courage to be an everyday hero.

IT'S ALL ABOUT THE BASS

Let's say you are listening to a song, and you are doing your best to shut down the sound of the bass. You want to listen to it all, except the bass. You replay the song over and over again, shutting your eyes, making a massive effort to hear everything in the song, but not the bass. No matter what you do, it doesn't work. Why can't you just shut down the bass from the song?

Well, we do something similar when it comes to listening to our universe. We invest massive amounts of energy into attempting to shut down what we don't want to hear; what we consider to criticism, judgment or attacks. We walk around, hearing it all, thinking that maybe we have some magic power to ignore and avoid what we consider unworthy of being heard and received.

What if this is the universe's way of showing us our blind spots? What if it was not judgment, but incredible love coming our way, helping us out to remove the ethereal spinach from our teeth? It takes so much bravery and courage to be humble enough to listen, to take it in, and to embrace the feedback coming our way.

Remember that the people around you are messengers from the universe. They are tools that, if they get enough out of the way, will allow wisdom to arrive for you. The more stubborn we are, the harder and more insistently the truth will be delivered.

You want to be whole-ass, and the universe tries to help you through the bass, yet you keep trying to shut the bass down.

It doesn't mean that you walk around believing everything you hear, and thinking that you are just a piece of crap. You are not. You are a human being, and therefore, as I have stated previously, you are a walking miracle. However, there is a magic formula for knowing whether or not what's coming to you has some truth in it:

If it sticks, if it hurts in some way, or if it makes you react and defend yourself, there is probably something for you in it.

See, in my country, there is a saying: "A palabras necias, oídos sordos." This means, literally, "Turn a deaf ear to foolish words."

There is no need to turn deaf ears when the comments flow through without sticking, and create no revolt inside you. In these cases, they simply go on, foolishly flying away until they probably smash themselves into a tree and disappear into thin air.

But you don't want to be deaf to the bass if you want to grow. No matter how many attempts it takes you, no matter how many times you've got to cry and whimper and squirm, you've gotta develop the ability to receive the wisdom and be willing to bring light to your own darkness.

Use your world for your own benefit. That's true courage. Embrace praise as well as what you consider criticism.

It is only the label you receive it under which makes it one thing or another.

I am no master of this, but I try every day. Why? Because there is so much freedom of being when you actually listen and take on board the hints from the universe, and grasp the opportunity to grow and evolve. You need to be free in order to be whole-ass, otherwise you are just limited-ass.

It takes much more power to resist, defend and justify your positions than to simply say, *"Thanks, and yes, I can be more of what you are suggesting."* Don't take my word for it, try it. It's true.

Real courage comes in every moment. It must become an inherent part of you.

Remember: it's all about the bass.

"Take the journey.
Take the lead.
Take the challenge.
Take the heat.
Take the first step.
Take the break.
Take the time.
Above all things...
Take the shot."

Kicking Horse Coffee

COURAGE TRAPS

THE LION'S TALE

"If I only had the nerve..." and the song from the *Wizard of Oz* plays in my head. *What an annoying lion! Grow some balls! Stop whining, you fearful wuss.* Oh, that lion got on my nerves when I watched that film. Yes, OK, he is cute and endearing and loving, but c´mon, man, you are the king of all beasts! He only needed what was probably a shot of tequila to start showing some courage. Thank God for the Wizard's smart-assness making him believe he had courage, because he actually did.

So, thanks to my reaction to the Cowardly Lion, every time I discover I am not being bold, I hear the tiny whiny voice inside my head say: *"If I only had the nerve..."* and that does it for me. I will not be that lion in this life.

There are so many areas in our lives where we play the lion's role. *"Oh, I would do that, but I'm too scared, so I won´t."* Let me tell you something, courageous people get scared, too, many times, but the difference is that they pull a John Wayne and do it anyway.

Fear is like a ghost. A whiny, wimpy, lying ghost that whispers in your ear what you can and cannot do. Fear tells you horror stories about what happens beyond its veil, and you buy it. You buy these ghost stories as if they are real; as if fear itself knows what lies ahead. Fear doesn't know what lies beyond itself. It is like a caged monster: it only knows it's box and nothing beyond it. It's never been let out, it's never known other lands and it doesn't know any other reality other than itself. Why? Because whenever that monster is let out, it becomes a shining angel.

Fear only exists within itself.

True dat. What lies beyond fear? Freedom. Expansion. Grace. Growth. A land of magic, fairies and elves, and whatever else you want. Beyond fear, the unknown becomes known, and is enjoyed. There are no limits to self-expansion and there is no time to succumb to fear, the same way there is no time to listen to a ghost talking about the land of the living.

The world doesn't owe you anything, and it won't hold your hand if you are not willing to step through your own comfort zone. Sorry to break this news to you, but there is no room for wimps.

However, if you are willing to do it, and more importantly, wanting to do it, there is help, always, everywhere. This universe supports courage.

NOT-SO-GREAT EXPECTATIONS

You put your astronaut helmet on, and you head outside for the first official rocket launch of the year. Everyone is there to watch you. It's a beautiful sunny day. Your palms are sweaty, and you've got the jitters. You were working on this all morning, after all!

The engine starts, what a sound!

All eyes on you, waiting for your stellar moment. You are the first of your generation to attempt this, you are so bold. The rocket slowly starts moving up, beating gravity. It starts building momentum, and soon you are going to disappear into the sky.

The sound stops, the rocket falls back to the ground and your mother yells from the kitchen that dinner is ready. All the kids at your birthday party run inside the house, leaving you, your rocket, your astronaut helmet and your pride outside, alone, sitting on the ground.

Something like that happens when the expectations of our dreams aren't met. We crumble. We worked so hard, building our rockets with such diligence and sharing each step with our loved ones. We get more and more excited, more and more ready, and then, sometimes, expectations and reality behave like two brothers in the middle of a massive quarrel. They just don't seem to want to shake hands.

So, our courage begins to fade, and we become less and less motivated to keep going, or to start another project that might end up smashing into the ground like the last one.

The thing is, we keep missing the point of trying to reach the goal. The point is to live with our whole-asses on the line at all times, and to absorb every drop life has to give us. Yes, you might attain the goal sometimes, but other times you won't reach it, and that needs to be OK for you. I do not make the rules; it is what it is.

Expectations can make us bump against reality so many times, we end up exhausted and wanting to be a couch potato for the rest of our lives. *Don't do it!* Keep going. Keep walking and building rockets, and getting excited about what might happen. That's where courage comes in.

Do it once and do it again. If it doesn't work, and your expectations or the expectations of others aren't met, do it again anyway.

Have clear goals and a blueprint for achieving them, but be open enough to be able to work with what life gives you back each passing moment.

Use life's inertia to your benefit.

Whether it is for a huge project or on day-to-day courageous attitudes, use life to your advantage. Yes, even when you gather all the courage needed to go talk to your boss, only to find that he is out of town, or when you are going to tell the person who holds your heart that you love them, and then when you arrive at their place, someone else has already beat you to it.

The fact that life doesn't match your current expectations doesn't mean that you are supposed to give up on them. Sometimes it's a matter of timing, sometimes it's a matter of finding a different entrance to the building and sometimes it's a very clear sign to change lanes.

The important thing is to make sure that the reason it didn't happen isn't because you didn't go for it.

Give it all and leave expectations outside.

Do it for yourself, speak up for yourself and embark upon what frightens you, for you. It takes courage to not allow unmet expectations to define your life.

LZ BOYS

Laziness and procrastination are the ultimate traps for courage.

Yes, you could do so many things and achieve so many dreams, but you just can't be bothered right now. Of course, you are courageous, just the other day you crossed a busy street without looking. How can you not be courageous?

Oh, well you forgot to mention that you crossed the street in that impetuous way because you had a massive attack of diarrhea after a curry night. It wasn't courage, it was pure necessity!

This is one of my favorite sins. I love doing nothing. My favorite days are the ones where I get to wear my pajamas all day, binge watch movies or TV shows, eat a good hamburger and sit on the couch until I force it to become memory foamed. I don't see anything wrong with that, as I am a firm believer that resting, like wandering, feeds creativity and productivity. However, sometimes, even I feel the urge to stand up and do something different, so I force myself to sit down and keep doing nothing, as if it were the most sacred of times. And sometimes, I can stretch the wonderful day for two or three more days.

There. That's my main trap.

And how does that affect my courage? Well, it keeps me in the gloomy world of the comfort zone. If I don't put myself on the line, then there is no line to jump, and therefore no need to use courage for anything. And courage comes when needed. It comes when we are putting ourselves in moments and positions that urge us to bring out our own strength and to be a better version of ourselves.

Procrastinating, and choosing to stay in the known, sedates our courage under a cloud of slow-me-down fog.

As courage is also a habit to develop, so is laziness. The lazier we are, the harder it becomes to start moving. The more courageous we become in our everyday life, the harder it becomes to overindulge in spending time hiding from the world or doing nothing but drawing clouds in thin air.

Again, when you are at the end of your life, which moments do you think you will remember? All those hours of incessantly scrolling through your phone, or those times where you felt alive, stretching yourself out into infinity?

"Ignorance is taught to you.
You were born in truth, from truth.
It is the mind-created structures
of the world that teach you
ignorance and limitation."

Narain Ishaya. Chit Happens. (2012)

Chapter 7

CONSCIOUSNESS

The Source of All Assness

We've explored the four aspects or habits that, according to my own life's research, a whole-ass person holds: Clarity, Commitment, Passion and Courage. But for me, the mother of all whole-assness, where everything collides and converges, happens when we turn our attention around and develop an intimate relationship with consciousness.

There are so many waves, trends, teachings, books, gurus, blogs and movements out there that apply the word consciousness to so many things. It has become a word that's mostly misused, and a concept completely misunderstood. Even though consciousness applies to every single thing under the sun, and is anything but a concept, it is THE thing to explore if we want to be real humans.

I will do my best attempt to define the indefinable, so that we are all on the same page when going through this chapter.

First of all, are you alive? I think it's best not to assume, and to instead start with the obvious question.

Are you a living, breathing mammal, defined as a human being, walking on Earth in the 21st century?

If your answer is "Yes," continue to the next question. If your answer is "No," I don't really know what to tell you. It's out of my range, sorry.

OK, you are alive.

Second question:

Do you think?

Do you have inside your head – you probably can't pinpoint exactly where – an incessant voice, which sounds like you and chats all the time, seemingly choosing the most annoying topics at the least opportune moments?

If your answer is "Yes," continue reading. If your answer is "No," you must be a completely awakened being.

Third question:

Do you have emotions?

These invisible trolls that seem to reside inside our bodies, even though they are not an organ, nor are they material. They appear sometimes for a reason, and at other times for no apparent reason at all. Sometimes they are happy trolls, sometimes angry trolls, and sometimes sad, miserable trolls.

If you do have emotions on a daily basis, keep reading. If you don't, please see a therapist.

Fourth question:

Do you see, hear, smell, taste and feel things that are in your surroundings?

Even if you are impaired in one or more of these senses, can you experience the world through the others? Do you know how a pepperoni pizza tastes? How does an apple pie smell? What's the color of the sky? How does The Beatles' Let it Be sound? How does the water feel against your body when you jump into a hot shower on a cold day?

If the answer is "Yes," you are on the right track. If the answer is "No," you might want to revisit your answer to the first question.

Fifth question:

How do you know the answer to the first four questions?

Who or what is aware of being alive, thinking, feeling and experiencing the world through the senses?

The obvious answer might be: *"Well, me, duh..."*

But who or what is that *you*? Are you aware of life happening when you are super-focused on a task, and you are not thinking about anything else? Are you aware of life happening when you are just chilling watching a TV show, with no real emotion swirling inside of you? Are you aware of life happening when your eyes are closed, or when you are eating?

If the answer to any of the previous questions is "Yes," then that "me" cannot be defined as:

a. A bunch of thoughts.

b. Emotional energy.

c. Senses.

d. A combination of the above.

So, who is the *"duh, me"* then?

Please don't judge me as a narcissist, but when I was a child I loved to spend a lot of time in the mirror, looking at myself. I would come really close, look straight into my own eyes and salute myself. I would tell myself things – I wish I could remember what the wise six-year-old version of me said – and I would explore myself; not my body or my image, but that alive, shining light that came out of my big brown eyes.

"Who is that behind the eyes?" Oh, that question!

Years after, if I looked closely at my reflection in any mirror, I could still find that same person behind my eyes. Regardless of my body having boobs and curves now, regardless of being a teenager with depressed thoughts and regardless of the emotion that was flowing through my body, the person behind the eyes was, and still is, the same.

The shine through the eyes, that is awareness. That is consciousness. That person who inhabits a space which seems to reside behind the eyeballs, experiencing whatever is happening in front, that is consciousness.

Let me tell you a secret. That person you have always been has always been peaceful, silent, still, joyful and eternally loving. That being exists beyond your thoughts and emotions; it's simply that they appear to be all too close to each other in our invisible insides, and we tend to mistake one for the other.

The real you doesn't change. It hasn't changed since you were a wee baby, and it won't change when you are all wrinkled up. Why do you exist? Why are you here? Why are you able to experience Earth? When did humanity begin? Will it end? How come you perceive situations in a completely different way to the person sitting beside you? What is all of this?

This is the game of Waking up. The consciousness that you are is constantly working holographically with the world around you, and you can always return home. The challenge is to stop identifying yourself as thoughts, emotions or senses, and instead recognize and live in the only space that is the real you: Consciousness.

WHOLE-ASS NOW

The real you is always present. Stop right now and look at whatever you have in front of you. Are you able to see it? Good. That reality is the only reality you have right now.

Now, stand up and walk to yesterday. Don't worry, I'll be here waiting for you to come back. What's that? You can't do it? How odd! You mean yesterday is not a reality right now? Interesting.

The same thing happens if I ask you to go to the future. You might say that you can go there with your imagination, and sure, you can, but is it real? Right now, is the future real? Can you look up and be in the future? Access to linear time is only a projection, so it doesn't matter if we go backward or forwards.

The way to access your consciousness is through the gateway of now, which is great news, because you don't have to go anywhere to access the biggest, and only real, part of yourself. You don't even need to get into your car to get there.

**Your consciousness is literally
closer than your next breath.**

Staying in the reality of now starts revealing your true self. Your true self is whole-ass by nature.

It doesn't want to miss a moment. It doesn't waste time with fears, excuses or rejection issues. It doesn't waste a split-second exploring the dead tenses, because it knows they don't even exist anymore. Ultimately, the way to create a perfect future is by creating a perfect present.

Once you are actually residing in the now, you'll see that there isn't a need to create anything, because the moment is already perfect. Yes, even that one when the waiter brings you cold lasagna. By taking this approach, you get to be a witness to this magnificent miracle in front of you: life.

You might think that you are always in the present moment because this is where your body is, and you might think that you are actually living your life because, hey, you are in it. But...

Where is your attention most of the time?

If your attention resides in the constant present, you have all the energy at your disposal because it's not being sucked up by imaginary dragons.

The most whole-ass people I know regard exploration of consciousness as their foundation, and that is no accident. This moment is the only playground you can actually be in. It is the only place that you can interact with, respond to and shape.

Try it. Go interact with the past or respond to the future. You can't. We have been conditioned to believe that reality resides in our thinking mind, but it's so simple to prove the opposite. No matter how many ideas you change, no matter how your beliefs and interpretations of life change during your life, the only tangible place you can actually be in is the present moment.

Whole-ass this moment forever, and it will result in you whole-assing your whole life.

The only way to give yourself fully to this moment, to be a total moment whole-asser, is by rewiring your attention and learning to keep it right here, right now.

It's really surprising to me when I see people craning their necks towards the floor, holding a device in their hands as they access a virtual reality, where only their sight and hearing are involved. We are constantly choosing to escape the present moment, to extract ourselves from it, and then we wonder why we long for connection and satisfaction.

The illusion of social media has us searching for fulfillment in yet another mirage. We keep painting perfection by posting pictures of a happy life, when in truth there have been challenges the whole week. We look for value in every single "Like" we get, and every comment received.

Have you ever tried to engage in conversation with someone who is looking at his or her phone? No matter how much they claim to be paying attention to you, you can feel that they're not even in the room!

I am aware that I am not saying anything new, nor am I looking to condemn the use of technology. I sure use it a lot myself, but I am stressing this point so that you can discover how life is lived fully by being completely present.

Life is full, the moment is so full, and yet you are not eating from it. You are constantly being distracted from the now, and then you go to bed wondering why you feel empty, no matter what you achieved during the day. You always feel hungry, but you can't eat at the deluxe buffet if you don't show up.

Being conscious is rediscovering the
ability to show up to your own life.

THE IMPORTANCE OF A PRACTICE

I don't know if I would've learned how to talk and walk if I'd been left to my own devices. Even the things I consider self-taught, I learned from a book or a video that another human being created in order to share the knowledge.

Every single thing we know, regardless of how true or untrue, we have learned from another human being. Even if you go into nature and observe and reflect on the behavior of animals, the way you process the information received, your own way of interpreting reality, was learned from either another person or from a community of people.

It only takes one quick trip to my hometown to remind me of how things that are considered unique in a different part of the world are just Average Joe occurrences where I'm from.

Everything is learned and we learn from others.

Learning to be conscious is no exception. A proper pathway – an established technique for accessing the moment, and with it your infinite consciousness – is imperative before you can begin to discover yourself. I use The Bright Path Ishayas' Ascension, and to me, obviously, it's the best. You are welcome to check it out or find one for yourself – just make sure it's a real deal.

I am a Photoshop aficionado, and I developed my skills by using tutorials, clicking buttons and screwing designs up. It's very common that I take two hours to achieve something, and then later discover there was a quicker, easier way to do it. When I see a proper designer, I am fascinated by the way they manage the program as a second skin. I kind of know how to use it, but I am no expert because I haven't invested enough time in it.

Something similar happens with consciousness.

A lot of us read books on self-help, consciousness, the Now or whatever else you want to call it, and then try to apply the information on our own. Yet the same filters we are trying to detach from are still filtering what we read!

You might have an idea of how to use it, or you might've memorized inspiring quotes, but the truth is that when your kid spills cereal all over the floor, just as you're attempting to leave for the most important meeting of the year, you forget all of your mantras and react very strongly. Being conscious requires a practice and live teaching. Walking alongside someone who has walked the path before you is what will enable you to permanently change your negative habits.

I found a practice in 2005, which I dove into fully in 2009. There were countless times where I would've distorted the technique and applied the practice incorrectly if it wasn't for the teachers that have walked ahead of me, and teach me again and again how simple and easy it is to be present.

If we can retrain the body, we can retrain our attention. Why the attention and not the mind, you ask? Ultimately, the thousands of thoughts we have every day wouldn't cause us stress if we didn't pay attention to them. The same goes for our emotions. Energy rises up, and immediately our attention shifts to it, and suddenly that emotional movement tints our reality.

When we retrain our attention to stay here, in the moment, in this reality, we no longer need to retrain our thought processes or our emotional world in order to discover peace.

*Retraining your attention is the best investment
you can make in yourself and others.*

The same way that we need a coach to train our bodies,
we also need a coach to train our attention.

My recommendation is to go get one. Find a true teaching
of consciousness, and enjoy learning through others who
have already done it.

> "The power of a car is separate from
> the way the car is driven."
>
> Edward de Bono.

"But why, Maharani? Why do you insist on this
consciousness thing? Why can't I just apply commitment,
clarity, passion and courage, and still be a true
whole-asser?"

Well, my dear grasshopper, it's very simple. Would you
rather jump into an empty pool or a full body of water?
Would you rather plant seeds in nutrient-rich soil or stale,
dried earth? Would you rather paint over an already
marked canvas, or would you prefer a brand-new, high-
quality, pristine one instead?

In case you are missing the analogy, you are the pool,
you are the soil and you are the canvas. My best friend
is a painter, and she has explained to me the importance
of the wood, the fabric and the quality of the paint. You
might be the most creative person in the world, but if
you paint over a shitty canvas or piece of scrap paper,

your creation will probably not endure, or be nearly as magnificent as it could have been. The paintings are your abilities and qualities you develop. Yes, you need high-quality paint if you want to have the best piece, but you also need a fresh, well-prepared canvas.

Becoming conscious is like becoming that canvas.

No matter how many tools you gain, or how many lists you make and how much effort you put in, if your machinery is filled with self-sabotaging habits, what you create will probably not be ideal. Looking in the direction of consciousness will provide you with a new self, clear of obstacles and limitations. Installing new habits there will make whatever you do blossom with very little effort.

THERE IS NO "I" IN WHOLE-ASS

Once you have a technique and a proper, proven pathway, growth becomes exponential. Every day you can make quantum leaps, and experience how your world reflects a cleaner, sharper, more loving vision of yourself.

You don't just grow once a year. You have the ability to expand your experience of yourself on a daily basis. When you discover that transcending judgment and limitation is simple, and that the rewards are boundless, then you can take every day, every passing moment, as an invitation to redirect your attention to your source of infinite power.

It's the ultimate game, and life becomes an endless adventure once you seize every opportunity to discover yourself as an entity that exists beyond the limitations of the mind.

I used to believe that growth meant I was doing something wrong, and for years I tried to change myself, constantly thinking I was flawed and in need of correction before I could experience life and happiness. I was forever looking for a glitch in the Matrix, to tweak it, change it and then see if I was finally doing it right this time.

Then, I learned to meditate, and through a lot of practice and willingness to let go of what I considered to be true, I discovered I am not flawed, and that growth presents itself on its own.

One of the most wonderful benefits of meditation is that the line between you and the rest of the world starts to fade. I've discovered that my world as I know it is always reflecting back where I am at. If I see love, understanding and joy, it's because that's where I'm at inside. Similarly, if I see lack, judgment and misunderstanding, that, too, is a reflection of my internal state. My world is not separate from me; there is no *they* or *I*. It's just one subjective experience that is always showing me what I am nursing inside.

That's how growth became joyful and effortless. When I discover a hidden pattern, or I start seeing reality as less than perfect, I now know that my attention has moved from infinite consciousness and is now entertaining a thought. It's so thrilling to know that the world is not against you, but rather that you're being shown how you are keeping yourself small.

As one of my dearest friends tells me: "Assume that you are doing great until told otherwise. Assume that you are heading in the right direction until life redirects you."

*The only common denominator
in your whole life is you.*

When you befriend your world and discover that the whole universe is here to support you, then you listen with no protection. You stop resisting what life is trying to tell you, because you know that no one is working against you.

It is a fascinating adventure, and no words can ever replace the experience of it; you need to see it for yourself. Unless your experience is one of love, joy, peace, unity and permanent perfection, you've still got a path to walk...

The most amazing path, back towards yourself.

"To one that is at peace, the entire world is an ocean of peace."

Maharishi Krishnananda Ishaya

CONSCIOUSNESS TRAPS

MENTALLY ENLIGHTENED

"We are all one, my friends. There is no spoon. Everything is love. Are you projecting? It's all perfect. There are no coincidences." You can install the brand-new Enlightenment 3.0 software in your mind, and still be a complete douche. Enlightenment is not about reading books and wearing beads and calling yourself spiritual.

It really doesn't matter what your mental software is made of, because enlightenment is actually the experiential recognition that you are not your mind and its construed identity of you. Some of us have spent so much time, energy and money reshaping our mental image of ourselves, not realizing that while it can help us be better people and have a better quality of life, it won't make us conscious.

This is a really scary trap, because a mentally enlightened one will not absorb wisdom with innocent eyes. On the contrary, everything he hears will be deflected with *"I know,"* or *"I know that, but certainly my fellow humans don't. They need this much more than I do,"* as he falls into half-assing the most important aspect of life.

> "HELLO! Look at me. HELLO! I am so ZEN. This is
> BLOOD. This is NOTHING. Hello. Everything is
> nothing, and it's so cool
> to be ENLIGHTENED. Like me."
> Chuck Palahniuk, Fight Club (1996)

Stating or thinking that *"I am enlightened"* is an impossibility. I mean, you are free to say it or think it, but it is and will always be a false statement.

You will never be enlightened, since it is in the awakened recognition that there is no such thing as an individual self that enlightenment can take place. Thinking that you are enlightened is simply adopting a spiritual identity. You can be a democrat, a vegan, a smoker and a spiritual. It's just another identity.

An enlightened being shows no external manifestation of their state. *"Oh but she is so enlightened, she wears cotton and doesn't eat meat.'* Nope, those are choices, not signs of enlightenment.

Yet, it's my experience that enlightenment is not as hard or as special as many people have been taught to believe. It's not only for a few chosen ones. If you have been born, you are entitled to wake up to the most humbling yet uplifting experience of being alive: the discovery that you are the universe itself. And you, or what you think *you* are, will dissolve in this discovery. What's left is pure bliss and everlasting fulfillment.

Read as much as you want, get excited and let your mind be open to a different possibility of life. But remember, gathering information about something will never replace the experience of it, the same way that gathering information about Hawaii will never replace the actual experience of being in Hawaii.

Mental enlightenment is one of the biggest contradictions a human being can fall into. No worries, though, for if you are brave enough to see that you have fallen into this half-assness, just remember that it's very simple to move away from it. Throw all knowledge away and become an empty vessel, primed for experience.

WHY SO SERIOUS?

Laughing at yourself is one of the most powerful methods of enjoying this life and the road to consciousness. Since waking up and discovering who you really are is of the utmost importance, it's very common to fall into the trap taking it, and thus yourself, so seriously that we completely miss the point.

We are going to screw up, that's for sure. We are going to take actions believing we are being so conscious, only to discover we've been just the opposite. We are going to be frustrated sometimes, upset at the fact that we're not getting this whole consciousness thing right. We are also going to believe that we are doing so well by not reacting through our old patterns, and then explode like mad popcorn one day and fall back into the same old shitty habits. We will do all of this, or at least 99% of us will.

And, who cares? None of us know how to live this moment properly. It is the first time we've lived it!

Every single moment, every single experience we are presented with, is always the first time. There is no moment in your life that you will be able to repeat; there is no *Groundhog Day*-type of experience in real life, and knowing this can put a lot of pressure on our shoulders as we attempt to be the best, most whole-ass version of ourselves.

At the same time, this recognition can help us cut ourselves a break and be gentle with our steps. Wouldn't you be gentle with a baby trying to take steps for the first time? Would you reprimand him and punish him if the second time he attempts to walk he stumbles and falls? No, of course you wouldn't, so why would you do it with your own being? Every moment you encounter is new.

Dare to fuck up.

The best medicine for taking life too seriously is simply laughing at yourself, and remembering that we are all just experimenting here. This game is not about doing it right or wrong, it's about choosing freedom or limitation. I love people who take themselves lightly. It's such a breath of fresh air, and a real source of inspiration to me.

My favorite friends are the ones I can laugh with, and certainly the ones that laugh at me when I am taking myself too seriously. Lightness propels the path by light years, and I can tell that it is only when I am really attached to my identity, and my idea of who I am or who I should be, that I take this whole deal seriously.

I am an Ishaya monk, and I have committed to walking the Path of Joy. So, imagine how ridiculous I look to my fellow monk friends when I start frowning and yapping about whatever. Seriousness doesn't last long in the presence of joy, let me tell you, and I am so grateful to be surrounded by these kinds of people. They help me see that I am just taking this moment with unnecessary seriousness, and immediately the ever-present consciousness of who I truly am grabs the wheel again once I relax.

Do you know another amazing thing that these wonderful people I surround myself with do? They let me fuck up. They are not concerned if I did things right or wrong, or if I was super-conscious or not. Countless times I've met with my spiritual teacher, feeling like a total failure because I was everything but conscious, and not once he has judged me for it.

A few months ago, I was in Spain working at the main meditation retreat that the Ishayas run. I had spent a couple of days feeling like a Gollum because I had doggedly held on to my positions, and had created huge issues with my boyfriend, who is also an Ishaya monk. On top of the fight, I felt like such a huge failure because there we were, two monks committed to joy, biting each other's heads off in the middle of a retreat, less than a mile away from our teacher. When the red mist clears and I realize I've screwed up, sometimes I tend to feel like crap for days, and this was definitely one of those occasions.

So, in a meeting with our Teacher, I shared with him how stuck I felt, in the same rut and the same Gollum state that I always fall into, and he told me: *"Well, in the past, your Gollum state would've lasted for at least a week. Now it lasts a day or two. How can you call that screwing up? You used to make it so hard for yourself, and after you gave us a good time and we got to laugh at you, now you are much kinder."*

Screwing up is a matter of perspective.

I GOT THIS

Arrogance is the mother of unconsciousness, and understanding is the father. This is a huge trap when it comes to walking the path of consciousness: *"I got it. I understand now. I got it all figured it out."* Just writing this makes me laugh!! I can hear the whole universe giggling when someone makes such a false statement, rubbing its hands, ready to lovingly prove that person wrong.

The thing is, we ain't got it. We never will.

There is no such thing as understanding life or the mystery of being here as human. You are welcome to try – God knows I have – but ultimately, the idea that we now know that A + B = C will constantly be proven incorrect further on in life.

As we start walking a spiritual path, we learn a few statements of truth, and our minds get all smug, thinking, *"I got this."* No, you don't. Put things in boxes and collect concepts as much as you want, but you will never get this.

Trying to figure out the intangible is doomed, and will forever keep you on the fence. We already spoke about the difference between gaining knowledge and experiencing something.

How can your feeble mind be so arrogant as to think that it understands the source of where everything comes from, and the underlying reality of everything that exists under and beyond the sun? It can't!

There have been many times where I've thought I have life figured out. I believed that if I had certain attributes, I would get certain results, only for it to come back and bite me in the ass. Whenever I think I've got it, guess what? I am such a half-ass in that moment, because I am refusing to see the whole spectrum of possibilities that lay in front of me.

I used to have a massive problem with being fair, or more specifically, life being fair. I thought that if I was fair, then I would be duly rewarded. Over and over again, I was proved wrong. It was so infuriating. Why is the world not responding to me if I am being the fair one? Why is God so mean as to not reward my just and fair self? Turns out, there is no celestial rule which states that if you are fair you will receive a good outcome. That's not the game here.

The game is to wake up, not to develop formulas for life.

There are no celestial rules. One time, you do one thing and get a certain result. Repeat it, and you might get the exact opposite. Life is constantly inviting us to not think we've got it.

Life is meant to be lived, not understood. One is active, whole-ass, while the other is passive and half-ass.

I wish I could tell you differently. I wish I could tell you that when you arrive at a certain stepping stone on your path to consciousness, you are handed a manual which tells you all the secrets to the mysteries of life, the world and the universe. I certainly wish that someone had handed a copy to me!

But the more you grow in consciousness, the less you know, and honestly, the less you want or need to know. You stop being arrogant, because you start recognizing that you are not the author of anything. You are a guest, invited to experience the magnificence of life. You stop trying to understand because every time you think you've got it, everything changes.

So, either you waste your time trying to understand life, or you focus on actually living it. Guess which one is going to take you to the end of your life thinking, *"Woah... what a ride!"*

PART 3

"You and you alone must
decide the life you want to live;
why not choose greatness?"

Maharishi Krishnananda Ishaya

Chapter 8

CHOP-CHOP

Get off your ass

OK, by now you hopefully have a pretty clear picture of what is it you want, and I really, really hope that you are all jacked up, wanting to take life by the horns and actually live.

And that is great.

My dream is to have as many souls as possible getting up off their couches and injecting their life force into this world. The irony here is that the greater the population, the less alive we are, but that is about to change.

Why? Because you are about to change it. How? Never stopping. Waking up every day with the full intention of experiencing and living your life's purpose.

You have a purpose. Each one of us has a purpose in this life. It's imperative that you discover it.

KEEP WALKING THE WALK

When I was a little girl, I thought I was special. I thought I was here to do something really important, really great. I did everything grandly. I don't know why, I just did it. I played big. I had a big role at school, in dancing, in being a bully, in being nice and caring, in unburying my family's secrets and in being dramatic.

I was just big. Mine was a tiny body with huge ideas.

When I was 13, I woke up one day feeling completely fed up with school. It was so boring to me. I would always download all this information on the first day of a class, and then the rest of the month I would just be bored to death, having to sit tight already knowing everything the teacher was saying.

One day, I woke up with an idea. I was going to ask if I could do the next year – 9th year – during the summer, so that I could start high school right away. I told my mom about it one late night, sitting on the floor by her bed, and she probably told me something like: *"Give it a try. I won't waste my time trying to dissuade you, because once you get something in your head, you won't stop."* She was right. I was that type of girl.

I arrived at school the next day, and immediately went and talked to the principal. She told me that even though at elementary school level this was possible, in junior high it wasn't the case.

I told her that I wanted an appointment with the head of the State Department of Education. I had been a perfect A student for as long as I could remember, and I seriously felt I was slowly dying inside, wasting all that time sitting in a classroom. I wanted to be a lawyer by the time I was 18.

Somehow, I got everyone on board and found myself talking to this dude. I told him exactly what I wanted and I got it. It took several meetings and a lot of paperwork, but it happened. The next summer, I took the annual tests for 9th grade and started High School at the age of 13. I was the first person in the history of the state to do this.

I woke up with this idea that came out of nowhere, and never doubted if I could or couldn't do it. I just did it. It didn't make sense, it had never been done and it seemed impossible, but no one stopped me, so I didn't stop. I owe a lot to that child who just knew that life would respond if she went for what she wanted, no questions asked.

The truth is, I started high school early and I flunked the semester. Ironic, huh? I just kept being bored, and I had discovered boys, cigarettes and cars. Who would want to be in a class when they already know the subject, and would rather be out there discovering life?

I wasn't an easy teenager. I was rebellious, manipulative, excessively emotional and completely lost. I tried to kill myself, I went to therapy, and for the love of God, I couldn't understand anything in life. It was like someone had turned off the switch.

After being a single-minded child with remarkable clarity at each step of the way, I was suddenly as lost as a mouse in a cat's house. Call it hormones, adolescence or just cosmic irony, but I ended up attending three different schools, I had messy experiences with boys and I could not figure out society. Oh, and I had a love for tequila and beer.

That girl who was so sure she had a divine purpose, and that life was on her side, was long gone. I still had to find out who I was and what I needed to do, and I did feel an extreme sense of urgency, but I went about it in such a messy way. Life didn't seem to like me too much, and I had this burning desire to find that *thing*, that reason why I was put here, and was now trapped in this teenager body in a middle-sized city, with a lot of strange societal rules.

By the time I managed to arrive, stumbling, at university, I had faded into the background. It was a school of 17,000 students, and I didn't talk in class for a year. No friends, no spark, no nothing. Just bronchitis after bronchitis, and drunken weekend after drunken weekend. School was still too easy for me, but that genius girl with dreams of becoming a lawyer and converting the Mexican legal system to oral trials had died. I was hiding behind 15 extra kilos and had given up, completely forgetting that I had a purpose.

And then I met a guy and I fell in love, madly. Eight months later, he broke up with me over the phone, and I died yet again. I was 20, and ready to go to another planet, refusing to accept that life was this thing where you are born, you suffer, you survive and you die.

Then, the sky cracked open, revealing a tiny glimmer of light, and somehow I started receiving help, as teachers of all different types began to appear. Finally, I remembered that I had a purpose which I needed to find. There was no time to lose.

"Chop-chop!" my heart said. "Chop-chop!"

Maybe you remember when you were a child and you had that feeling, or maybe you don't. Maybe you, too, settled and gave up on life. Maybe you are still searching now. Whatever your situation, I would like you to know that you have a reason for being here. You are supposed to be alive and to know happiness, and to utilize this in the service of others.

Yes, *you*.

Do not stop until you find your divine purpose.

How will you find it? It will show up if you keep moving. It will start revealing itself once you start whole-assing every single moment. Even when you get discouraged, even when life doesn't make sense and even when it seems you are been thrown in a completely different direction.

Sometimes, what you do will make perfect sense, and other times it won't. Sometimes, it will seem that you are friends with the world, and other times it won't. Sometimes, you will be extremely clear about what it is you want, but there will also be occasions where you'll feel lost.

The courage to keep walking creates miracles, opens up doors and allows magic to occur. It's easy to engage life when everything seems to be going smoothly. The trick is engaging it with the same momentum when it all seems to be conspiring against you.

> **You were born to be great, so let the greatness of life shine through you.**

Not for a single moment should you doubt this. Your purpose is to wake up from the illusion and, in the process of becoming conscious, start living with the intention of having an impact in this world.

ACTION PRECEDES MOTIVATION

"Oh, but I don't know what to do, so I am waiting for inspiration so that I can actually get in motion."

Let me get this straight. You are sitting on your couch, binge-watching TV shows and hoping that maybe Jon Snow is going to look at you, very *The Office*-like, and tell you exactly what to do, so that you can get all geared up and head out the door?

Laziness generates more laziness.
Action generates more action.

I know all about being lazy. I guess it's a remnant of being so bored of having all the time in the world, when doing assignments required such little effort. I learned to enjoy doing nothing and being a couch potato, because I constantly felt I was being held back by life, and also because I spent so much time at home fighting bronchitis.

Left to my own devices, sometimes I could slip into La-La Land and lose a whole week doing nothing. And guess what? The lazier I get, the harder it becomes to get back into action.

Last year, I went through a period of having no clue what to do. I felt I had all this passion inside me, but I didn't know where to direct it. I was waiting and waiting and waiting for inspiration to show up at my door and tell me what to do. Months passed, the passion was eating me up, but I just kept waiting for that divine inspiration, totally stuck.

Being completely fed up, I started moving along what appeared to be the path I needed to follow. Still a bit unsure, I decided to put all my stones into going back to acting. I didn't know why, but it was the only thing that made sense in terms of having a great impact in this world.

I was living at the beach, so this change entailed moving to Mexico City, taking acting classes again and then starting to find my way into film. Once I was a well-known actress, I reasoned, I would have the proper platform to let the world know that life is much more than we think, and to share the conscious message with the world. An actress-monk. It sounded so cool!

So, I started taking steps towards that. I got some headshots, made phone calls and started talking about it. I started searching for apartments in Mexico City, and my plan was to move there in the summer, after I'd finished at the retreats where I usually work as a translator for my spiritual teacher.

At the first retreat of the season, I told my teacher about my plan. I knew that if I was serious about it, I had to let go of the translation gigs that usually took up three or four months of the year.

You can't be in two boats at the same time.

I knew I couldn't attempt to do both things, because then I would half-ass them both, but it seemed so hard to let go of my role on the retreats, as I loved it so much. I had a lingering idea, nagging away in the back of my head, that being *just* a translator wasn't big enough, and my teacher told me: *"If you are going to go after that, you shouldn't postpone it. Come to Spain for only a month, instead of the usual two."*

I panicked.

I kept walking and following through until I arrived at another retreat, where suddenly it became so clear that I did not want to get back to acting and leave this behind.

All this time, I felt I wasn't doing enough or being big enough, and I worried that my role in life was too small. However, through a series of conversations and clarity hits, I saw clearly that I was exactly where I wanted to be, and that all my actions should be directed towards this.

I wasn't just a translator. I am blessed enough to serve as the Spanish-speaking voice for the most conscious man I have ever met. It's because of my work that hundreds of people get to receive his message, while I receive the benefits of spending a lot of time with him, and learning and living in the midst of a multicultural, vibrant community that certainly knows how to have fun.

I closed the acting door for good right then and there, and it felt as though my energy became as straight and true as a pointed spear.

I left to go to Europe for six weeks, and ended up staying for six months. After Spain, I went to Italy and started writing this book, along with a lovely guy, also a writer, who became my boyfriend. I then got the opportunity to teach at retreats in Norway and on courses in England, before later returning to Spain. Life has been non-stop action and motivation ever since.

The lesson is that I needed to start moving, even without motivation or absolute clarity. I needed to start shaking that ass and walk. In the middle of these actions, I received motivation, and in my case, the motivation was directed towards a completely different path.

So, don't wait for motivation to come. Start walking towards something, even if it's just a tiny idea.

Do not wait to have all the cards laid out in front of you, since life is rarely that straightforward. The path usually lights up step by step, and sometimes there are things happening in the background that won't present themselves until the time is right. Sometimes, we are only able to see in retrospect the series of events that led us to stand in front of something we wanted.

"Oh, so THIS needed to happen for THAT to happen, and then that other THAT to happen. Duh!"

It's a brilliant piece of machinery, this universe thing. Your steps are the indicators that tell the machinery to unleash certain aspects into your life.

Set your world in motion.

"The ancient one: you cannot
beat a river into submission.
You have to surrender to its current
and use its power as your own.
Dr. Strange: i control
it by surrendering control?
That doesn't make any sense.
The ancient one: not everything does.
Not everything has to. Your intellect
has taken you far in life,
but it will take you no further.
Surrender, Stephen. Silence your
ego and your power will rise."

Dr. Strange (2016)

PAY ATTENTION TO WILL

Once you start moving, you need to pay attention to Will. You have your will, and then there is the Will – that unseen force which somehow seems to come and rearrange everything so that it falls where it should.

Many of our conflicts come from the fight – which is useless, I might add – between our will and the Will. We want things to be as we think they should be, and we want them to look as we think they need to look. We act as individual islands against the forces of nature, attempting to stop rain when it's pouring and trying to blow wind when it's obviously still.

Want to give it a try and attempt to stop the waves from coming?

We do not stand a chance against the Will.

You might fight and moan and push and resist, but life will keep trying to tell you where you actually have to go. The less you listen, the louder life gets, but this doesn't mean that it's working against you! *Au contraire, mon ami*, life is always, always, always trying to support you. It's us, and our stubborn ears and limited perspectives, that think we need to fight against what is.

It's a *pas de deux*. It's a beautiful duet, where you hold life by the waist and let it lead you. You move your feet, too; you learn the steps and attempt to be as graceful possible, but you dance together, not against each other. Anything else is futile and will look awkward.

When you start walking, you need to pay attention. Let the Will become present and dance with it. The reason why this is so much fun is because there are no rules. Things not flowing smoothly doesn't necessarily mean that you're never supposed to go that way.

One time, I asked my teacher how I could know if I was being clear in following my path, or if I was trying to impose my own will. He told me that trying to impose my own will feels like carrying a wheelbarrow up the hill.

Personal will is not a bad thing at all, but learning to be aware of the Will makes the road ahead much smoother, quicker and way more exciting.

I am usually a very willful person. If I want something, I don't stop until I find a way to get it. I look at the situation from all possible angles until I find a way, which more often than not is invisible to normal eyes. I don't think that's a flaw, but an asset. When my heart believes in something, I'll do anything in my power to make it happen.

However, sometimes I've missed the signs, not listened to the universe and then ended up distraught and destroyed, wondering what hit me. It's only when I've looked at it in retrospect that I've seen, so freaking clearly, how life was trying, constantly, to tap me on the shoulder and tell me, *"Dude, not that way!"*

It happened to me with Gardenia Guy. My heart was set on him, and straight away I *knew* he was the One I had been searching for my whole life. I saw our future together, and there wasn't one tiny ounce of doubt.

And I went for it, whole-ass. Although, maybe a better way of putting it would be all-ass, no brains.

There was nothing that could distract me from it. I was willing to do what needed to be done to make it work, because my heart was right. Move cities, compromise and even darken the truth so that he wouldn't feel uncomfortable around me. I received warnings from the universe from day one, but I kept on ignoring them.

The Will kept trying to show me a different way, and I kept flicking it. I even got fat. Well, not fat, but I gained a significant amount of weight in a not-so-significant amount of time. I'd look at photographs and not recognize myself, but I kept ignoring it. He was constantly telling me all the reasons why we wouldn't work, constantly showing that he was half-ass with me, but I just kept making excuses for him. Everything stopped flowing: work, courses, traveling, etc.

And me? I was ignoring it all, walking with my own will in mind, completely attached to the outcome I had in my head. I was even willing to let go of my own dreams and desires in life and settle for a tiny existence, just because of this "certainty" I felt one day.

One afternoon at 5pm, I was lying on my couch, watching a TV show when I realized that my life had become: cook breakfast, watch shows, cook lunch, work a little, watch more shows and then go out to visit him at work. Eat. Drink. Sleep. I clearly remember having the fleeting thought: *"Is this my miraculous life? Is this it?"*

Of course, I ignored it. Why? Because of my will and wanting to prove myself right. Because my certainty wasn't necessarily an intuition hit so much as it was a way of holding on to love outside of myself. He represented the love I needed to look for within.

Luckily, two weeks later he broke up with me.

I remember clearly that, as he was breaking up with me, my experience was one of perfection. There was peace and nothing more. The way I interpreted it was: *"Well, this means we are getting back together. He just needs some time to see the truth."* Ha!

Still not getting it! And that's the danger of trying to impose your will on the Will. You just don't see because you don't want to. Angels can come down and tell you syllable by syllable exactly where to go, and big red signs can smack you in the head, but if you are in it, you will not see.

Ultimately, you are only making it harder on yourself by delaying the inevitable.

In case you are concerned about my sad, sad story, I eventually I snapped out of it all and moved on with my life. Now, I am so immensely happy and grateful to understand that at certain times we are all completely and utterly wrong.

And that's OK, because the Will had greater, better, more magical and miraculous things in store for me than my tiny baby mind and its will could even comprehend.

So, go for what you want with all your heart. Really.

But do it as if you know that:

*The whole universe is working for you.

*You need to be open to the possibility of being "wrong" and changing course.

*There is a greater Will out there, and the more you get out of the way, the more you align with it.

*Befriending the Universe doesn't make you lazy, and it doesn't mean that what you do is not big or important. It means that you are humble enough to accept all possible help.

YOUR FRIEND INTUITION

What's the best way to listen to Will? Through your intuition, of course! We all know intuition, and I believe strongly that in the near future, it will be taught in schools much like rational thinking is. At least I hope that's what happens.

Intuition is your divine GPS.

Intuition is what allows the Will to communicate with you. It's an instant knowingness, a certainty that something will go a certain way, or that you need to turn left when you are supposed to go right. Intuition is that thing which tells you to call someone you haven't seen in ages, exactly when they are having a bad time.

One time, when I was planning my move to Barcelona, a friend of mine asked me: "Where on Earth do you get your ideas from? It always seems you are going a certain way, and then it's like you jump lanes and go off in a completely different reality and direction."

I'd never thought about it before, and when he said it, I was like: *"Hmm, I don't really know. They just drop to my head."*

That's intuition – an instant hit of something, and not a long speech in your head or a rational process. It's as if you are connected to the highest speed Wi-Fi on Earth, and you can receive a full download in an instant.

Lots of works of art come that way. Artists can relate to intuition because they know how suddenly, while grocery shopping, they get the next painting in their head. It's the same even scientists, as it's not when they are working and working and analyzing that they find the solution to a problem, but rather when they go for a walk and rest their minds that they see it.

We are not responsible for it, but we can become increasingly in tune with it. Trust your intuition more and more. It's never wrong.

I remember one time, a long, long time ago, I was trapped in Calgary for a few months. I had no money, no house and no idea how to survive in the world of humans. I was a distraught fairy in a foreign country.

Luckily, I met two incredible Canadian girls, and we became friends in a heartbeat. They opened their homes to me, and eventually I was adopted by a group of Australian guys that were spending a year working in Canada.

At that time, I was really into reading about spirituality, and was reading a book on intuition. I would try and play with every single thing I read, from trying to manifest my thoughts into reality to invoking magic wherever I went.

I was surviving well by doing random tarot readings here and there, and one day, in the summer time, we all went to this huge event in Calgary known as Stampede, which was a rodeo-like cowboy event, with games, concerts, poker tournaments, etc.

I decided to break off from the group when we first arrived, because I didn't want to walk around and drink a lot. I wanted to sit down and read. Yes, I know that's weird, but that's who I was.

When one of my friends asked, *"Mate, how are we going to find you?"* I replied, *"I will find you. I am sure we will meet each other."* They kind of looked at me as if they were never going to see me again and then left.

This was 2005, so I might remind you that there were no smartphones.

Later that evening, I was ready to find my friends. There was a huge venue within the venue that you had to pay to get into, and a concert was about to begin. I left my passport with the guard so that I could go in to look for my friends. I don't know how, but I knew there were inside there.

I walked in and saw a huge arena with thousands of people sitting beside one another, and second crowd stood occupying the space between the stage and those that were sitting. It was like an enormous rodeo.

I walked in and immediately felt the panic running through my body. *"How on earth am I going to find these dudes?!"* But I was determined to put into use all my learning about intuition.

As I kept walking and looking using my rational mind, I became more and more annoyed, and I was convinced that this had been a terrible idea. The stakes were high, because if I didn't find them, I wouldn't have a home to go to.

Then I stopped. I stopped using my thoughts and my mind, and also stopped actively looking. I went into this "flow" state, letting my body move to where it actually wanted to go, and opening space for myself between the standing crowd.

Less than a minute later, in the middle of thousands of people, I found my friends. Their jaws dropped and the concert began.

Intuition is perfect and flawless. More often than not, we just keep getting in our own way and end up taking the longest road.

> "This world is built on magic, not rocks."
> MSI

DO YOU BELIEVE IN MAGIC?

I love magic. I think it is as real and tangible as the house next door. Have you ever seen a video of how a baby is created in the womb, or how the human body works? Call it sophisticated science, or call it magic.

Eventually, both ends - science and magic - will meet and laugh at the centuries of human nonsense, and our stubborn attempts at positioning these two on different sides of the spectrum.

Magic is everywhere around us, if only we are willing to see it. I remember being a child and my dad playing that trick of removing the thumb from his hand. *"Oh my God, magic!"* Of course, now I know it's just a trick, but in that moment my perception was of magic.

Change your perceptions, and magic will appear again. However, it will not show itself if you don't believe. Peter Pan knew this, and now so do you.

We can sometimes be very arrogant in thinking that our reality is the only type that exists in this world, but that is really far from the truth.

Some people have the ability to spend $10,000 on a dinner with friends on any given day, and then afterwards hop aboard their private plane and head to a different part of the world. Do you think that their reality is the same as yours?

My boyfriend is Scottish, and I, as you know, am Mexican. He has lived in both Australia and England, and he regularly travels the world. I have lived in Canada and Spain, and I also travel a lot. These are similar lifestyles, yes, but as we interact and get to know each other, we discover so many differences in the realities we have built for ourselves. There are so many instances where, because something us true for us, we assume it must be true for everyone else, too. It becomes hilarious sometimes!

From rules of etiquette and what is considered normal, to meanings of words and what we judge to be "logical" in any given situation. And this is from two people that have moved around the world and have explored other cultures and ways of being.

Imagine one who has never left the same spot. They, too, believe that everyone else's reality out there in the world is the same as theirs. It's the same thing with magic.

There are people out there who deal with magic on a daily basis. When I say magic, I refer to sacred objects that hold power, such as extremely secret machines that heal the human body. There are alternate realities, ghosts, visions, healers, shamans, spells and more. There are people who bend time and space, and impact the collective consciousness by changing their own reality; and there are those who transform the atoms in a room just by entering it. All of these people exist in this world, and they have a completely different reality to yours. You can believe or not, it doesn't matter. It's all real, and don't even get me started on aliens, because that's the same thing.

You will only see what you are willing to see, and it would be so sad if you were to limit your potential to see beyond what you already know.

We are all wizards.

We are wizards, but we are too distracted to look into our own power. What are we scared of? Who is preventing us from living every day in the most wonderful way? No one really, other than our own minds. We are unlimited. We are boundless. We hear this 1000 times, yet we don't allow ourselves to believe that we would find a parking spot at the supermarket, if we only sent some magic dust a few miles ahead before we get there.

If you are capable of experiencing the unlimited on the inside, it makes sense that it can also be reflected on the outside, don't you think?

Before I became an Ishaya, I was strongly linked with magic. I would meet up with my friends and play, and I am not talking about when I was 10 here, but when I was 25. We would spin around each other to elevate our vibrations, we would read our energy fields, we would bring desires to the table and make them happen. We would heal just by looking into each other's eyes, or pull cards and speak about our powers as super-humans. We would bring up the unconscious and make it known, and sometimes we could see into each other's past lives.

None of us had a Wicca background, and God knows we had no idea how we were doing it, but we believed in magic, and yes, our days were completely magical. Also, I thought I was a fairy in human form, but that is yet to be proven.

When I discovered the Silence, I dropped all that side of my universe, labeling it as new age, and something that didn't "go" with the Ishaya life. This served me immensely, because I needed to put my feet on the ground and become comfortable in this reality, but then time passed and magic came back into my life.

Magic makes everything more fun.

A dull day can become absolutely fantastic if you believe it so. When you want to park your car, invoke magic and find the perfect spot. When you want a piece of furniture, embrace the magic and see how it comes to you in the most spellbinding way. Play with changing the weather, send some telepathy to your boss to give you extra vacations or spin your atoms clockwise. Wake up every morning knowing that magic will be present all day long.

Who cares if it happens or not? The idea is to bring back the childlike wonder into your life. This world is built on magic, and only clean eyes can see it.

One of the things I love most about meditation is that it impacts the rest of humanity. Every time you transcend a limiting thought, you move one step closer on behalf of everyone in the world who is struggling with it. There is only one collective consciousness, so whatever you put in or take out of it impacts everyone else. I am not a quantum physicist, but I am sure it can be explained in scientific terms.

Every time we Ascend, we are doing the most magical thing of all and healing this world by impacting everyone's thoughts. When we gracefully employ these techniques, it seeds the possibility in the hearts of lots of people, telling them that there is a choice and freedom is real. One more heart lights up each time, and there is nothing more magical than that!

It makes you wanna gear up and live life for the rest, and if you feel sometimes like living for the rest is too much of a responsibility, think of this:

Did Batman ever got too lazy to hop in the Batmobile? Heck no!

BE AWARE OF DISTRACTIONS

One thing you learn when you are into meditation is how much your mind gets distracted. The mind is like an ADHD kid high on sugar: it keeps moving and pulling in different directions, never content with what it has right now.

I would sit down to meditate, and 30 seconds into it I would go to the bathroom. I would come back and, one minute later I would be grabbing a pillow and a blanket because it's cold. Come back, and two minutes later I would be in the kitchen getting a glass of water. Five minutes later, after almost getting into it, I would check my phone because I might be receiving an important message. Four minutes later, I decide to get up and go take a shower because I need to RIGHT NOW.

Get the picture?

Now, something you learn in acting school is rising up the stakes. The higher the stakes in the scene, the richer the acting will be.

Let's say you have to deliver some papers to the guy who's coming at 2pm. If those papers were a pizza discount, you would not care less if you actually gave them to him, and you might even miss the appointment. But, if those papers were the proof of a wire transfer you made so that the mafia would release your sister and her life was at stake, and the guy you were meeting was a mafia messenger, you would do anything in your power to make the appointment and hand those papers over. Would a phone call distract you? No. Would getting a drink distract you? Probably, or at least hopefully, not!

The higher the stakes, the less likely we are to get distracted.

Distractions are a wonderful way to half-ass our lives, our current project and our search for enlightenment. You are walking with all your heart towards your goal, and somehow you lose half a year because you were distracted by life. Suddenly, all these urgent things seem to appear, and the truly important things are pushed to the back of the line.

How distracted would you be if you were running late to take a flight to meet the love of your life, who you hadn't seen in four years?

You wouldn't be distracted at all.

Cultivating that same attitude towards everything we do is whole-ass meat. If an actor can learn it, so can you. Remember, most of the ways we approach life are just habits, and cultivating the right habits will enable us to lead a whole-ass existence.

HANDS ON ASS 9: THE DISTRACTION

Notice, in an hour, how many times can you get distracted.

Set yourself a task: write a story, paint something or fix your drawers. It doesn't have to be long. Just set a task and start it. Pay attention to the urge of distraction, or note down all the times you can actually get distracted. Pay attention to how many "important" things you think about. Pay attention how many times you check out by thinking about something else.

By becoming aware of our distractions, we can start being more and more focused.

Everything you do is important. No matter if you are washing dishes or creating a sculpture. Everything you do deserves your full attention.

Give your entire day the attention it deserves. All of it.

CURIOSITY KILLED THE CAT... ONLY TO BRING IT BACK

Curiosity is the salt and pepper of kicking ass. It will keep you going forever, embarking on adventure after adventure.

I am an extremely curious person. I love investigating, watching and discovering more things in my own way. Like, I am not curious about running one of those ultramarathons, but I would love to be present at an open-heart surgery. I don't want to be the one on the table, obviously, but I'd love to observe first-hand what the doctor does to a live human body.

I am life curious, too. I am curious about human emotions, human limitations and the confines of the mind, so much so that when I was younger, I thought at one point that I was going a bit insane due to the amount of existentialism I was pondering.

Too many times it got me trouble. Too many times I said yes when I was surely meant to say no. I ended up hurt, or in chaos, or hurting someone else. (I don't think I am doing such a good job of selling you curiosity here!)

Curiosity also brought me a shitload of wisdom, while providing me with experience of testing boundaries on my own. I started building my own useful limits, instead of believing there was an imaginary fence around me. It has taught me a lot about humans and how we are all so different, as well as what does and doesn't moves us. The source of my curiosity lies within human nature.

Where does yours lie? It could be nature, mechanics, travel, engineering, cooking or chemistry – anything really.

What makes you wonder, and makes you want to walk one more step?

My dad is a great example of the benefits of being super-curious. He loves knowing how things work, and his observational capacity is such that it is very simple for him to figure out pretty much anything, while sometimes expecting all of us around him to follow at his pace! He loves life and is super curious about it, and whenever he has kind of dominated something, he immediately finds something else that challenges him.

He learned to fly airplanes when he turned 60, and got his pilot license and a little plane. He just keeps going and exploring, and is genuinely interested in any new things that cross his path.

That is an extremely blessed trait to have.

Curiosity brings enjoyment up to the maximum. It is the engine which powers life. When was the last time you got curious watching ants doing their job? When was the last time you stopped and watched the birds fly around? Do you know how they communicate, or why they can fly so perfectly? When was the last time you looked up the origins and meaning of a word just because it fascinated you? Do you know how a telephone really works? Do you know why we say yes when we want to say no? Do you know what makes airplanes fly? Do you know what's on that street that you always want to walk up, but for some reason never do? Do you know how it feels to try that pottery class?

There are no limits or overdoses
with curiosity. Use it every day.

"I'm not sure what the future holds, but I do know that I'm going to be positive and not wake up feeling desperate. As my dad said: 'Nic, it is what it is. It's not what it should have been, not what it could have been, it is what it is'."

Nicole Kidman

Chapter 9

POKER FACE
Play the cards you're dealt

I like to see life as an extension of myself. It's the wisest mother one could ever ask for, who sometimes gives us a nudge, and other times a big smack in the head when we are not taking the hint.

It is patient as it guides us on our journey, and it also has more wisdom and a way bigger field of vision than our limited viewpoints allow.

Many times, I've found myself fighting against it. I come up with an idea, I lock myself in a specific vision and, like a bull, I tend to walk towards it without paying attention to the road. More than once I've fallen off a cliff, not because I am ballsy, but because I didn't see it.

So, it's very important to remain aware and attentive to what life is presenting to us. We must have our desires, our commitment and our motivation to go, and be super open to the cards we are given.

IT IS WHAT IT IS

My favorite coffee mug says exactly that. Man, I hated this sentence for as long as I can remember, and now I love it.

A few years ago, on a winter's day, I decided to take a shower at around 6pm. It was really cold outside, so I closed the bathroom door, turned on the hot water and got into the shower. Boy, it was delicious. My partner was due home soon, so I wanted to be all fresh and clean and to cook him some dinner.

The house was really old. It was a downtown construction, circa 1910, with one of those inner patios. Very vintage-y, very hipster-y; I loved it. But, being an old house, it had many imperfections, one of which being that the bathroom door sometimes got stuck for no reason. I am sure there was a genuine reason, but when it came to my abstract head, it was just a moody door.

My boyfriend had taught me how to unstick it by pushing the doorknob down with all your body weight before turning it. Easy!

So, after my shower, I grabbed a towel and tried to open the door, but it wouldn't budge. I laughed and tried again. Nope. *Nada.* I then got annoyed at my boyfriend for not just fixing the door, and attempted one more time to open it. The room was filled with steam by this point, and I hadn't taken any clothes or my phone in with me.

I couldn´t follow the whole "push down the doorknob" instruction, because I was shorter than him and needed a stool, so I sat on the toilet and meditated. My initial amusement had turned into a bit of anxiety, after I'd kept trying with all my strength but still couldn't open it. I saw a butter knife on the sink – God knows why we had it in there – and I thought that maybe unscrewing the doorknob would work. Luckily, I stopped halfway through executing that idea, when I realized that it would´ve left me stuck in there for good.

It would have really just been a harmless mistake, except it brought all sorts of anxiety symptoms with it. The thought of being stuck crept through my whole system and I couldn´t breathe.

I tried to get some air, but there was only a tiny window by the shower. My mind started going out of control, my body went into panic mode and everything became foggy. In a desperate state, I started pulling the door, naked and scared, with all my strength.

One, two, three, four, five pulls, and still nothing.

I tried again, and finally the door opened. I was free. I walked to the bed and lay on it, and then I started crying and called my boyfriend. By the end of the night, we were both laughing about it, and I never gave it a second thought and kept living my life.

Around two weeks later, it was Christmas. We spent the holidays with my boyfriend's parents, and although I had a terrible cold, I was determined to have a good time. During dinner, I started feeling weird, disconnected, scared and short of breath. It was really, really weird, and I thought I must have been OD'ing on ginger or something. It passed after a few minutes.

Long story short, I started having these episodes everywhere: in the car, at the mall, in my house and at parties. I would start freaking out and feel like I was going to disappear from the face of the Earth. I would start shaking and fighting it. I started seeing the common thread: wherever there was the potential of being locked up and trapped, my body would lose it. If I was driving my car and I suddenly found myself in a traffic jam, my body would get into fight or flight mode. I would start exploring exit routes, trying to locate nearby hospitals and would start shaking uncontrollably if I got stuck for a while.

Then there came the day when I had to take a flight. I am used to flying, and I've always loved it, ever since I was six years old. The plane took off, and while I was up in the air the thought flew by: *"What if something happens and I need to get off the plane right away?"*

I want you to know that I understand the irrationality of it all. Even while this was happening, I knew it didn't make sense. I knew that everything was OK, that the plane was already in the air and that my head was just going crazy. But my body couldn't help itself – freaking panic attacks! After a couple of years, it would take me weeks just to book a flight, and if I could help it, I would choose drive long distances rather than get on a flight.

Trust me, this doesn't work at all when you spend two months of every year in Spain!

I was so mad at myself. I am a meditation teacher, who teaches people how to transcend the mind, and there I was being a complete slave to it, without being able to find the way out. Eventually, the episodes started diminishing and I was slowly feeling normal again, but I was still in no position to fly without hearing screaming inside my head and sweating from head to toe.

I began to discover that the more I fought with reality, the more this shit went on. I was constantly fighting with what is, and wasting time wishing that things were different – that I could have a more zen and less strange life. But the more I accepted things as they were in the moments that they were happening, the quicker these problems left my body and the less broken I felt.

It's our judgment of what is
that creates a problem.

I wasn't broken, nor was I failing as a teacher. Do you know how many people I've since been able to help, when they were going through a similar experience? Dozens. It took me years to recognize that I didn't ask for that experience, nor did I do something wrong.

I would try to accept "what is" by convincing myself that I was already on a plane, that this was the reality and that I should accept the fact that I couldn't get out while I was in the air. What I couldn't accept very well was having a massive internal meltdown. I was fighting with something that was already happening: my mind freaking out on a plane. First, I needed to be OK with feeling anxious and panicky.

And that's what I did.

Remember how you would feel the night before the first day of school after summer vacation? You knew that the next day you were going to feel nervous and jittery, but because you assumed it was normal, you didn't give it much importance. I started to handle the panic attacks in the same way. Why? Because my best friend and eternal plane coach, who would always be there on the other side of the phone to help me through, told me: *"Just pretend it's normal. It's the norm to feel like that when you hop on a plane."*

For some strange reason, it worked!

Last year, life started opening up opportunities to transcend this phobia for good, and with a lot of help I started walking towards that. It's not fun to live in fear and feel limited!

I am immensely grateful that now, when I book my flights and hop on the plane, I feel normal. Like, real normal.

It all began with accepting what is.

Life has a way of presenting you with different challenges to spice up your experience, and to maybe throw in a few twists and turns where you thought there was a straight road. Even your emotions and your body do the same thing.

***Accepting what is enables you to work
with life and not against it.***

Do whatever you want, but it is what it is. The road is already closed, the shop doesn't have your perfume, your partner doesn't cook well, *Game of Thrones* ended that way and you simply don't have long legs. It is what it is.

How is this going to help your warrior self go out and whole-ass life? By letting you change things from a space of acceptance, and not from resistance.

BREAK ON THROUGH TO THE OTHER SIDE

Acceptance is becoming friends with what is. Resistance is like an electric fence that surrounds your identity, and goes off whenever there is an attempt made to cross it.

There is the potential to confuse resistance with clarity. We can convince ourselves that our uncomfortable feelings – those ones which make us squirm when we are faced with our patterns – is actually our intuition speaking.

But many times, it isn't. It is just plain old resistance.

We tend to resist:

a.   What we don't like.

b.   What we don't understand.

c.   What is unknown to us.

d.   What is different.

e.   What makes us feel uncomfortable.

Where there is resistance, there is the potential for growth.

If you are really serious about this whole-ass thing, you need to be willing to let go of any resistance you encounter along your path. Why? Because behind your points of resistance, there might actually be a faster route to a greater path; an ideal outcome and a potential new you.

And c'mon, by now you probably know for yourself that whatever you resist will simply persist.

Do you honestly think that you keep recreating the same type of relationships because you have bad luck, like it's the number you got at bingo? Sorry to burst your bubble, but it doesn't work that way.

Anything you resist will keep showing up in your life again and again, until finally you see it for what it is and let it go. Life doesn't care if you are on a path towards consciousness, or whether or not you want to be whole-ass. It works the way it does because it loves you.

HANDS ON ASS 10: THE RESISTANCE

OK, so think about recurrent themes in your life. Either you are constantly trapped in long processes that make you feel like you are losing your mind, or you always end up having turbulent vacations. You are the type of person that always gets their food order coming back wrong, and it gets to you every time.

What is it about the things you resist that represent a problem? You hate messy people, and guess what? You end up always surrounded by them!

Write down the things you resist about yourself: sleeping late, not being able to speak up, your straight hair.

Now write down the situations you resist the most in your life: being on your own, when people don't listen to you, when you can't do what you really want to do.

Are you able to see that it is your judgment of what happens that represents a problem?

Once we know our resistances, it becomes easier to recognize them when they appear and then walk straight through them.

I know people who would carry around doubts about something in their life rather than ask a simple question. And guess what happens? They usually end up in situations where the only way they can get clear on something is if they ask.

Every time you resist something, there are two choices. You either break through the resistance, to where freedom lies, or you stay put, let the uncomfortable feelings pass and then wait until it happens again. It *will* happen again, no doubt about it.

Have you ever been afraid of doing something for years, and then on the day you decided to finally do it, you discovered that it wasn't so bad after all? You had this list of excuses why your resistance was justified, which you have been adding to over the years. The mind is so clever that way. Remember:

> ***Resistance is the electrified fence***
> ***that keeps you in your safe zone.***

By the way, resistance is not this evil mechanism designed to sabotage your whole-ass existence. None of our habits are. Resistance is merely a survival mechanism. It has helped the human race survive and evolve over many, many eras.

Resistance makes you second-guess if it's safe to throw yourself from a 10th floor. Resistance used to help you be quiet when speaking up meant you'd get beaten up in other lifetimes, or sent to jail or hanged. But the more we evolve as a race, the more we are safe in our environment, which means the more resistance becomes useless.

As we mature in consciousness, we start recognizing that what hurt us when we were children does not necessarily hurt us now. If, when you were a child, you spoke up at home and you got beaten up by your parents, that does not mean you will get the same again.

The more you fill yourself with love, and the more you love life, the more confident you will feel in transcending resistance.

And as my wise teacher says: "No resistance equals freedom."

Take as many leaps as you can. Life becomes so enjoyable! The more I transcend resistance, the more I want to. Would you have learned to ride a bicycle? Would you have done a presentation at a theater? Would you have told that special person your feelings for them? Would you have studied for a Master's degree at 45? Would you have changed your emotional habits? Would you have seen life through a broader vision if it wasn't for the fact that you have stepped through resistance probably more times than you are aware of?

It's within you. You are much better-equipped to soar and transcend than you might give yourself credit for. Why else would you be attracted to the title of a book called *WHOLE-ASS*?

Our inner spirit never ceases to burn. We are designed to be free, and to allow everything to come up without resistance, be they feelings, thoughts, actions or situations. Holding nothing makes us free and light. The more you train that muscle, the more resistance in every other area of your life dissolves.

And then one day, you become like air. Nothing to resist and nothing to fight; letting life flow through.

The more experiences you allow, the more they will come, until every day becomes this wonderful adventure. Soon, you'll recognize that instead of resisting something, you simply say, *"Woohoo!"* and jump over it.

Life is an extreme sport.

IT'S ALL ABOUT THE MIRROR, ALICE

Your world is like a Nintendo game. The cards you are dealt are a constant reflection of where you are at.

Please do me a favor and try not to intellectualize this concept:

It's all a reflection of you. Your world and you are the same thing. It's not just a projection. It is you.

Imagine you were a game designer, pitching the following game to Nintendo:

"So, there is this main character named Yu, and Yu was born in this planet, Earth. Then there are all the other characters that Yu interacts with: the family, the colleagues, the store clerks, etc.

"What Yu doesn't know is that all these people are not really independent entities, and that they all respond to Yu's patterns, and the concepts that he has picked up during his upbringing. Sort of speaking, they are all an extension of Yu.

"For example, and this is just an example, his mother voices his doubts, while his father speaks his cheerleader thoughts. His kids represent the innocence that he lacks sometimes, and his wife represents his most secret fears and illusions. When he was growing up, he felt as if he would disturb his parents, so generally speaking, he feels like that when he is around people, and he sees through a filter which perpetuates this feeling.

"Everyone represents an aspect of him. It's all just a big mirror."

"So, what's the game? How does Yu win?" the designers ask.

"The game is that Yu, through his interactions with the mirror, gets to a point where he is tired of recreating the same thing over and over again, and thinks: 'Well, there's gotta be something more to life than this!'

"So, other characters start appearing, or even the same characters start behaving differently. Yu stops blaming the outside world for his life and his feelings. Yu recognizes that in every single moment, his existence is attempting to show him how he has believed all his life that he is the product of a bunch of thoughts and emotions. The whole universe is attempting to show him that he is loved, fully.

"Yu begins to discover that the more he lets go of patterns and finds peace within, the more the other characters change towards him. It appears as if all the characters have changed overnight, but truly it is that Yu has changed his perception by starting to identify more and more with the Silence within. This allows the other characters to change.

"Yu recognizes that he is the source of peace or suffering, and that he is the motor which powers the world into change. Yu recognizes that he, through his perception, can either create a standard reality or the ultimate reality: Heaven on Earth.

"Ultimately, Mr Designer, that's the goal – Yu discovering through the mirror that Heaven is right here on Earth, right now. And once he discovers it, the game continues, because he also represents an aspect of the mirror to the other characters. They start reflecting on him, and where they used to see sadness, now the see love; where they used to receive judgment, now they see neutrality. A part of them starts remembering, and a sparkle is ignited. They start wondering if there is something more to life than recreating the same thing over and over again... thus their game begins."

I don't really know how well this game would do in the actual world, but I find it a fun way to explain how this whole holographic world works, and how you can use it to recognize that you are not separate from your world, but rather that it's an extension of you. It works for you as an infinite outpouring of love, constantly highlighting what you think you are in order for you to leap in consciousness and fill the gaps with love and infinite peace.

As my wise Teacher once told us:

"You want to grow fast and wake up soon? Stop resisting parts of your universe. Stop selecting reflections and taking only the ones that you consider 'conscious.' Your universe is all of it. All of it is parts of you, guiding you where to go and what to let go of. ALL of it. If you want to wake up soon, be wide open to all of it."

"Only a life lived for others
is a life worthwhile."

Albert Einstein

Chapter 10

SERVED WITH A SMILE
Give it all

You've got the backpack, you've got the tent and you've got the truck. Now you just need the route.

Throughout this book, you've seen if and where you are half-assing. You have become clear, committed, passionate and courageous, practicing all of these elements ahead of integrating them into your daily life. Then you got a hint, a divine hint, on the importance of waking up from the illusion of being limited beings, in order to be a full on, moment-to-moment whole-ass. You also got a few tips on how to befriend the world and kick ass.

Now, where are all these going to be applied? Where can you direct all of these newly learned abilities? Honestly, wherever you want. Be whole-ass about whatever the fly you want – when you are cooking, when you are planning a vacation and when you are taking a walk in the morning. Be whole-ass with your neighbors and your boss. The more things you whole-ass, the more you will want to whole-ass your whole life.

However, I would love to suggest something:

To be fully and completely whole-ass means to give yourself fully to your life; to serve, to give and to find ways to improve your surroundings. This world needs people who are less about themselves and more about serving, with the goal of helping to make the world a better place.

> "If you want happiness for an hour, take a nap.
>
> If you want happiness for a day, go fishing.
>
> If you want happiness for a year, inherit a fortune.
>
> If you want happiness for a lifetime, help somebody."
>
> Chinese Proverb

Sometimes we try to help from a space of scarcity, seeing only that the vase is broken. It can never work that way. We need to see things in their perfection in order to create change, and for that, we need to see ourselves in perfection.

At least this is how I understand Albert Einstein's wise words: "A new type of thinking is essential if mankind is to survive and move toward higher levels."

We need to rise above the mind frame that created the problem in the first place. See someone as broken, and you will never give them the opportunity to see themselves in a different light. The only way to see things in a different light is by changing our own perception of the subject in question.

Making the world a better place can only begin with you. Heal yourself fully, since it's in the eyes of the beholder that perfection lies.

That's why it's so important to start with ourselves; to see ourselves first, to become conscious and then, from that platform, help the world do the same. Rebuild it in your flavor, with your own passion and with the one thing YOU are designed to do.

Living in service is a wonderful way of being. Not to feel noble or better, or to put yourself on a pedestal, but because serving is in our nature; it truly is.

My dad always told me that I shouldn't look for a career with a focus on making money. He always encouraged me to find a service – one that I am passionate about – to my fellow humans, and that abundance will follow.

When you serve with passion and joy, you get out of your own self, you stop thinking about your poor life and you instantly set yourself in the present moment.

I am very lucky that most of my time is spent among Ishaya monks. Now, don't go imagining a monastery in the Himalayas, where we all dress robes and are sat around in silence. That's exactly what I thought when I first heard of Ishayas, too!

Ishayas are modern monks. We live all kinds of different lives as housewives, doctors, lawyers, architects, artists, coaches, you name it. However, we all have something in common: we have committed our lives to healing humanity by healing ourselves first.

How do we heal ourselves? By waking up. From what? From the illusion that we are the limited part of ourselves, the temporary part. How? By living.

It is not what we do in our life that changes once we become monks; it is how we do it and how we relate to daily life. We go through a thorough meditation-based training program, which teaches us to change our relationships with our minds, our emotions and our bodies, and then off we go to engage life and practice our techniques.

It's easy to be at peace hiding in a cave, but the true challenge is discovering that the same inner peace exists when you're having coffee with your high school friends. We would be of no service to humanity if we stayed in a cave forever. Not in this lifetime.

There are many things that we continuously learn on our path, and one of them is the importance of giving. Being in service all the time? Does that mean we don't ever have a good time ourselves? No. Does that mean we do not get to be pampered? No.

When I serve at the retreats as a translator, I get to share a household with other Ishayas that are working there. It's such a blessing to experience that type of living. Everyone is always out to give, and there is a natural flow when it comes to household chores like cooking and cleaning. That's how you end up always giving and always receiving at the same time. The more you receive, the more you feel compelled to give.

Giving is the healthiest addiction.

Have you ever prepared a surprise for someone? If not, I highly recommend that you do so. For whatever reason, just do it. If this is something you have done before, you might relate to the fact that often you, the *surpriser*, get as much out of it as the *surpriseé, if not more.*

There is so much excitement and rush, creating true feelings of well-being. It doesn't matter if you simply pay for a stranger's soda in the supermarket, or if you plan a huge, grandly-produced surprise... honestly, it just feels great. You should really try it.

This is no science book, but it's been studied and proposed that giving activates the areas of pleasure in the brain, and produces both oxytocin and serotonin. It has also been suggested that generosity is part of our natural behavioral patterns as human beings.

> "Why not simply honor your parents, love your children, help your brothers and sisters, be faithful to your friends, care for your mate with devotion, complete your work cooperatively and joyfully, assume responsibility for problems, practice virtue without first demanding it of others, understand the highest truths yet retain an ordinary manner?"
>
> Hua Hu Ching: The Unknown Teachings
> of Lao Tzu as translated by Brian Walker (2009)

GOOD ON YA, MATE.
AND YA... AND YA!

One of the easiest, simplest and most powerful ways to give is to praise. No, I am not suggesting you go to church and sing and pray to an apparent God outside of you. That is not the type of praise I'm referring to. I am talking about the simple art of appreciation.

I don't know how it is in your world, but in the one I grew up in, complaining and criticism were much more prevalent than praise. I would constantly hear what I did wrong, what the neighbor did wrong and what the bad news was during a conversation at any given table. If you did something right, it was forgotten tomorrow, whereas if you did something wrong, it followed you around for years and would be used as a conversation starter as you were introduced to new people.

Growing up, I was constantly startled by this. Becoming a teenager and trying to fit into social groups was the weirdest, most alien transition my human body has ever experienced. My usual thought was: *"What the fuck is wrong with these people?"*

I was forever hearing about the lives of random people who I didn't even know. If you didn't know who they were, then you were probably a nobody. Everyone's life was scrutinized if they dared to do something mildly outside the established social rules.

So, I did what I had to, being this new teenager with new boobs (real, not fake) just trying to fit in. If they gossiped, I gossiped. If they drank, I drank. But I was always too honest, too transparent, and guess what? Too nice! True story: one Sunday I was waiting for my friends to pick me up, and they never arrived. There were no cell phones in 1996, so I just stood there, like a cactus, waiting. My so-called friends stopped including me in their circle without so much as two weeks' notice.

I won't tell you how devastated I was, but you can put two and two together. Fourteen-year-old + no friends = disaster. I believed that something was seriously wrong with me. One day, out of the blue, my three girlfriends came to see me. They asked me to forgive them and they said that they missed me. When I asked them what had happened, their response was the most ludicrous thing I'd heard in my short life: the guys that they used to hang out with, who I met through them, told my friends that I was just too nice of a girl. Not a goodie-goodie, but nice. As in, I would tell them nice things about themselves, or appreciate them and the moments or situations. Bottom line, I was too praiseful.

I would be lying if I told you that this didn't affect me, and negatively impact my future behavior. From then on, I would always display a "Fuck you!" attitude at first, and you would not see my softer side unless you were a really good friend.

I cannot begin to stress how important praise is in this world.

We live in a world where bullying is normal. Kids at school can be incredibly mean. Why would you bully someone? You pick the reason: for being short, a different color, for wearing glasses, for being poor, for liking studies, for being sensitive, for being ugly, or fat or just because it turns out you were sitting in the wrong seat on the first day of school.

Early in life, negative thoughts and mental bullying constantly impact kids. If it's not directed at them specifically, they hear it between their parents or on TV, and nowadays they read it in social media comments.

A long time ago, someone shared with me a study done by PhD students in Iowa, discussing the family lives of farmers.

These students visited the farms and observed the family dynamics all day long. They were studying the relationship between parents and their children, and because they were taking their samples from what they perceived to be simple farm folk, the expectation was that it would lean heavily towards the positive side. However, the results were as follows:

The children received, on average, 400 negative comments a day, e.g. *"You are an idiot, you will never get it,"* or *"You always do things wrong,"* or *"You are too slow."* By comparison, the daily positive comments amounted to just 37 on average.

Going by those numbers, that works out at up to 144,000 negative impressions on the kid's brain per year. Multiply that over, say, 18 years, and you get 2,592,000 negative impressions in their little brains!

What happens to these kids? Eventually, they don't get hurt by the comments anymore; they just assume that that's the way it is, and it becomes their standard. They grow up with underlying feelings of having little self-worth, wondering why they can't live a happy life or achieve their dreams. They give up on the idea of a wonderful life before theirs even begins. They settle for less without even trying for more, because they don't see themselves as worthy, capable, etc.

No wonder there are five-year-old bullies and 50-year-old bullies. After all, we are just little kids running around in adult suits.

Now, imagine a different view. Imagine that we all grow up in a household filled with praise, appreciation and motivation. Imagine people at dining tables talking about the great things someone has done or said that week. Imagine that the front pages of newspapers always shared the most amazing, groundbreaking, positive stories. Imagine that people didn't gossip, because for gossip to exist we would first need criticism.

Imagine that we would change the lives of everyone we encounter, for the better.

It doesn't take being a Mother Theresa. All it takes is for you to educate yourself, rewire your brain and start praising.

You see, the magic of it is that praise is something you can choose to engage in. In every single moment and experience in your life, you can choose whether to judge or to praise.

If it's a restaurant, a conversation, a bad experience or even a case of standing in front of someone who has hurt you, you can find something to praise.

Giving praise is free, by the way, so don't be cheap with it. You truly never know whose life you could save just by noticing them, and then giving them a reason to feel good about themselves. You might help with those 2,592,000 negative impressions that most people already have.

Happy people equals happy world. Do your part.

Also, praise has the power to change the energy in a room, to stop an argument or to flip the side of the coin. I dare you to praise someone and frown at the same time.

In my hometown, there is a woman who has made it her life's purpose to create a newspaper and a TV program that only shares good news. I find that amazing. Against all odds, she has reached many people, and does her service to society by giving some healthy brain food and a different perspective to whoever wants to wake up with a different feeling in their gut. There are so many different ways to praise; what's yours?

HANDS ON ASS 11: THE PRAISE

Incorporate praise into your daily routine. Decide to do it for one day to begin with.

Praise any time you can. Praise whoever makes your breakfast. Praise someone for opening the door for you. Praise the clerk if you go to the shop.

You don´t have to praise what they are doing, or only if they are doing something for you. You can praise their eyes, their headband, their jacket or their smile.

Praise your co-workers, praise your partner and praise your kids.

Explore what happens to them when you praise them, and explore what happens to you when you praise them, too!

Do not expect any praise in return. This is your mission.

After one day, you probably won't want to stop... so don't.

AND WHEN YOU CAN'T POSSIBLY GIVE MORE...

... you guessed right...

... give more still!

Sometimes, we fall into the trap of feeling low and believing that life doesn't like us very much, and that we have nothing to give. We think, *"How am I supposed to go and help someone if I feel like shit?"*

The truth is, if you were at your lowest point, and then suddenly your neighbor's house crumbled to the ground, and some of your neighbors were trapped underneath, you would jump out of your misery and start helping. Do you think you would even remember how awful life is, or how lonely you are? Probably not. You would be in action, giving, serving. Technically, using this premise, you are physically capable of giving at any given time.

It kinda works the opposite way to what you'd expect. If you feel you have nothing to give, then give. Start giving wherever you can. Make a phone call and offer help. Help your household by making breakfast. Brush someone's hair. I don't care what you do, just set in motion that giving motor, and next thing you know, you won't even remember why you were so full of self-pity.

There is no such thing as not having anything to give, unless you are dead, and even then, I keep receiving the most amazing gifts from my mother in all different ways. Sometimes I even wonder if she is maybe alive, hiding on a remote island. If my dead mother can give, you can, too.

Don't be deceived by the idea that some people are naturally giving, while others just aren't. True, maybe it comes more natural to some, but giving can be a learned trait. It's also a habit, and the more attention you give it, the more it grows; the more it grows, the more contagious it becomes. These are the epidemics that we need now.

> "I slept and I dreamed that life is all joy.
> I woke and I saw that life is all service.
> I served and I saw that service is joy."
>
> Kahlil Gibran

There is another magic trick for giving. It can help how you view a situation, especially when it comes to relationships. My teacher taught me it a few years ago, during a series of arguments I was having with my boyfriend at the time.

Let's say we would get into an argument. My tendency was to be mad at him, so nothing would come from my side to him. I was so justified in my position that I could only see what was wrong with him and the relationship. Everything seemed so dull and doomed to fail. It was hard to get out of that loop, and almost impossible to view him under the light of love. *"Once we fix this, I'll be normal again. Once we overcome this, I am sure I will see him in a good light again."*

I was constantly expecting him or the situation to change, and for me to feel good about it again.

Luckily, I talked to my Teacher about it, and he advised me to give. "Even if you don't feel like it, even if no part of you wants to give and praise right now, do it. It will change the energy. Unless, of course, you prefer to be right more than to be at peace, then, by all means, stick to your guns." He always teases me that way whenever I don't get the lesson. "And do it with no expectations of him, or even the situation, ever changing."

Begrudgingly, I would do it. I would start cooking a special meal, for example, to surprise him, and inevitably I would start getting feelings of love and well-being. Oh, so annoying! I would get more and more excited, and by the time he came home, I would be so happy to see him that I'd have almost forgotten the problem. Nothing had changed on the outside, or with the situation itself, but when my attention moved to giving, I naturally focused on the love instead of the problems. From a loving place, the situation would naturally arrive at a solution.

Other times, I would have to praise either him or the situation. I was very reluctant at first, and mainly just doing it because my teacher told me to, but eventually I started to see for myself how this attitude would dissolve arguments, help me see through my patterns and allow solutions for our interactions to happen more quickly.

Now, I do it almost instantly. I am not saying that I don't argue with my current partner, as we are both very pig headed, but the next day, with that feeling of yuckiness still lingering, I make an extra conscious effort to be praiseful, kind and giving. No longer can I be the victim of circumstances, nor can I wait until things get better on their own. With this attitude, you give relationships the best chance of not drifting into the abyss or being dissolved by silly arguments.

This applies not only in romantic relationships, but also in all relationships; not only in arguments, but also in the good times. It applies to any tricky circumstances.

An attitude of giving and serving
helps solutions to appear.

As my teacher told me: "Even if you are going to leave the relationship, leave giving. Give until the last possible moment."

HANDS ON ASS 12: THE SERVICE

Yep. Serve. Give.

Find all possible ways to give today.

Again, with no expectations of getting anything in return. You are doing this for you, not for anybody else.

Notice how giving and serving also engages you more with life, with your reality, and makes you connect and notice more of what is happening around you. Serving gets you out of your head and makes you part of the whole.

Serve joyfully.

"Everybody can be great... Because anybody can serve. You don't have to have a college degree to serve. You don't have to make your subject and verb agree to serve. You only need a heart full of grace. A soul generated by love."

Martin Luther King, Jr.

SWEET-ASS

"He who wants to do good,
knocks at the gate; he who
loves finds the gates open."

R. Tagore

Whole-Ass is not a book of power. It is a book of love.

Eating the world up and living life to the fullest doesn't mean running over people and having no regard for the fact that we are part of a collective.

It's one thing not caring what other people think, especially when their opinions are based on fear of the unknown or blind criticism, but it's something completely different to believe that we are an entity detached from the rest of the world. What we do, or don't do, has an effect on the rest of humanity.

If your foot moves to walk, your whole body goes with it. Even if they all have different functions, all of our cells work as one single organism. If our liver cells went on strike, the rest of our body would perish.

As much as we may like to think that we came into to this world alone and alone we will die, and that we don't need any help, or are in no way connected to the rest of humanity, quite the opposite is true. Otherwise, how were you born? Did you just appear here? No, you needed at least two other humans, and for them to be here, they needed two humans each, and so on.

Everything we do, or don't do, has an impact on the rest of humanity.

This might feel like an extreme burden or a great honor, depending on how you choose to view it. If you want to be happy and joyful, I would suggest going with honor. It is what it is. It doesn't have to be hard and it's happening anyway, so we might as well put it on and make the best of it.

Now, if you are a hurt little dove, you might be thinking: *"Screw everyone, I don't care if my actions affect them. They all can go to Hell."* Well, first of all, if absolutely everyone went to Hell – if Hell actually existed – you wouldn't last very long on Earth, so that's not very smart. Secondly, no matter how hurt you feel now, or how many times humans have proved themselves not worthy of you, the truth is, you were, are and will be forever loved.

YOU ARE LOVED.

No matter what you do, the sun comes out and shines for you. Even if it is behind the clouds, the sun is still providing all its nourishment for your body. Without the Sun, you would perish. The sun never wakes up and thinks, *"Man, I am totally annoyed at Susan today. I am just not going to work for her today, screw her."* No matter how much you have blamed, cursed and hated the sun on a really hot summer day, it always loves you. It's simply its nature.

Your nature is also love, and so is everyone else's. Even Hitler just wanted to be an artist before being rejected by the Academy of Fine Arts in Vienna, and becoming whatever it was that he became later on. He was love, only he was covered in so much dust that he totally lost it.

The advantage of plants, for example, is that they cannot think. Thus, they cannot hide their true nature behind filters, perceptions and unforgiving pain, and then one of these days start denying us fruit just because we are so mean to them.

I am not a plant, so I don't know if they can become consciously aware of being love and being loved. I am, however, a human being, and I sure know that it's not only possible, but also our divine right to recognize that the only thing that exists, the only true state of being, is pure love.

Regardless of what I say, it's almost impossible for me to prove my point with arguments, so hopefully you can feel in your beating heart that proof of love is everywhere you look.

I recently watched the Netflix show *Narcos*. I was really hesitant at first, since it's a story about drug dealers, and we have enough of that real-life story in my country, but when I started watching it, I was amazed by how great it was. Even that dude Pablo Escobar, having killed so many people and infected so many others with all the drugs he produced, was absolutely in love with his family and his close friends. He wasn't a loner and he wasn't pure evil. He was just another man who valued power above love, but he, too, loved and was loved.

How many of the things that we do or don't do are to experience love? The search for approval, validation and recognition are rooted in a craving to experience love, the most addictive of all emotions.

How many attitudes do we develop that prevent us from being hurt again? Perhaps we believe we can only be hurt again if we experience love? If we were icebergs, hurt wouldn't exist in our vocabulary. So, strangely, we try to stop ourselves from experiencing love while at the same time it is the very thing we crave the most.

Trust me, I've tried it. It doesn't serve anyone, this whole *"I won't love again"* façade. This baggage makes your path heavy and dusty, and it definitely holds you back. So, it would be a great thing to do to clear your baggage and start forgiving anything or anyone that's gone unforgiven in your past.

A TALE OF FORGIVENESS

This forgiveness thing can bring up so many attitudes of pride and so-called self-respect. Well, if you really respected yourself, you wouldn't want to walk around carrying grudges and old pain. You are too precious for that.

Ultimately, every single thing you have lived – the good, bad and ugly – has brought you to this point. Change one tiny thing in your life, and you will probably be in a completely different reality.

A long, long time ago, when I was 14, I was madly in love with a boy. He was 16. The first time I saw him, I was driving around with my friends and he was standing outside someone's house with other boys. We drove by and I saw him. I felt my heart stopping, probably for the first time.

"Who was that guy?" I asked my friends, as if my life depended on the answer. No one knew who I'd seen out of the bunch of guys, so no one could tell me. Then, like two weeks later, I saw him at a club (yes, I was a precocious

teenager). He was quiet, and I never saw him smiling or being an obnoxious teenager like the rest. My friend told me his name, and for the sake of this book, let's call him Random.

So, I had a name and I had a face, but I was too shy to even get physically close to him. So, I just looked at him, and then looked at him some more. I was smitten. He took my breath away.

A week or two after that, me and my friends went to a fair, which was an annual thing in my city, and we ran into some of Random's friends. At this point in our teenage lives, we had never hung out with this group of guys before, but somehow that night we all ended up hanging out, and agreed to meet the next day to do something fun. My house was a social center, so they agreed to pop by the next night to hang out.

The next night, the doorbell rang and my friends went downstairs to open it. I was finishing my hair or putting on a summer dress or whatever, and when I came downstairs and opened the door, there was Random himself. Other people were there, too, but they all faded into the background once I saw him.

How on Earth was he delivered to my front door? I have no clue. Was it the power of attraction? Was it that I noticed him because somehow my inner self knew he was going to become someone important in the near future? I have no idea, but there he was, and we were finally properly introduced.

He was shy, and he didn't look too interested in trying to score with a girl like the rest of the boys. We kept hanging out with that crowd for the following month, and at first he showed no interest in me at all. So, I started going out with his cousin, the charming one, until he broke my heart and left me for his ex. In the meantime, Random and I became really good friends.

My friends and I went to the beach to celebrate my 15th birthday, and Random and some of his cousins – not the heartbreaking one, others – were *coincidentally* going to be there the same week. My crush had passed, and now I just thought of him as a fun friend.

I ran into him one evening, and he grabbed me for a dance. Then he kissed me, and my whole world turned upside down. For the rest of the week, we spent almost every night together, clubbing, hanging out at the beach and saying goodbye after 2am. He lent me his ring – the one he never took off, which had belonged to the father who had abandoned him – as a token of his real feelings for me.

When we got back to the city, the gossip started. His friends told me he didn't care for me at all, so next time I saw him we had a big fight – one of those sitcom fights where everyone is yelling at the same time, until he shouted that he loved me and everyone went quiet. We made up and walked back home.

He was still shy and weird, but I loved him. We saw each other a few more times until one day he left for a school trip and came back with an official girlfriend.

My whole world collapsed. I was 15, existential and felt completely unloved and abandoned by the universe. I wrote more than 100 poems for him, and he became my whole purpose in life. I am not proud of it, but that's the way it was.

The next summer, we ran into each other at the same beach town, and he grabbed me to dance and we kissed. I thought I was back in his life, and that he'd discovered how much he loved me. I had been playing with some white magic to bring him back, which I thought was working! After what happened next, kids, please don't play with that at home.

We went to the beach, and everything started going south from there. He wanted more than kissing and I didn't, so a struggle began. The more I said no, the more he was trying to force himself on me, and we fought for a while until I felt disconnected from my body and became resigned to whatever was going to happen. There was no rational computing of what was happening in that moment.

Then, my friends passed by the beach and I used the reverse psychology trick. I asked him to stop while they walked by, and told him we would keep going when they left. Luckily, he did, and as soon as he got off me, I stood up and yelled at him. I walked back to my room with my dress half-torn, in complete shock.

There were so many psychological setbacks and traumas after that: fear of love, of opening up, of men, of trusting. You name it, I had it. It showed up in the most random and incoherent ways. My teenage world became really ugly when word on the street was that I was a slut and I had slept with him, so a lot of boys would approach me to see if they could get me into bed.

The strangest thing was that for the longest time, I never felt any type of hatred in my heart for him. There was this weird knowingness that it all happened for a reason, and that I didn't have to forgive him since there was nothing to forgive. Honestly, in my experience, there was only love. There was an enormous amount of pain, but love nonetheless.

My friends nailed me for this. They drilled into my head that I didn't love myself and that I needed to hate him, to be proud and to never look at him again. I ended up even more confused and layered up than before. I both loved him and had been hurt by him. I couldn't understand why he would do something like that to me. I still loved him, but at the same time I hated him. Boy, I tell you, it took me a few years to get out of that one!

The more I wanted to hold on to those feelings of, *"never forgiving him until the day I die,"* the more life seemed to reject that attitude.

One time, at a soccer World Cup - the one with Ricky Martin's song - Mexico won a game and we all went celebrating. Me, my friends and my boyfriend were crossing the street, and some paramedics stopped us to let other paramedics pass by with an injured person. The paramedics stopped to open the ambulance door, and there, lying down right in front of me, was Random. He had been in an accident and had broken a bone. He was at his lowest, and what he saw was me. I felt nothing but concern for him, but my head told me to ignore it and to gloat. To my friends I was gloating, but not to myself.

Six months after that, his mother died. I went to the funeral, not caring what other people would think of me being there, and that almost ended my two-year relationship with my boyfriend. He couldn't believe how I humiliated myself just to go and pay my respects, but I couldn't not go. Someone's mother just died.

Around a year later, I was driving back with a friend from the club, late at night, in a sketchy part of town, and a car rear-ended me and then sped away. I was still discombobulated, trying to figure out what just happened, when Random appeared at my side window and asked if I was OK. He was driving right behind me, and stopped to help me through the whole process. His friends left him there, and we drove him to his house once the whole thing was done.

Life kept putting us in extreme circumstances where unforgiveness couldn't exist.

Another five years passed, and I had moved from the city. I had moved on with my life, yet that specific event would come and bite me in the ass, especially when it came to sex and feeling guilty, dirty and not at all able to enjoy a healthy sex life.

One time, I came back home for a few months and had recently discovered weed. I called a friend, and he told me about this other friend that smoked weed, so we went to this friend's house and I ran into an old high school friend. There we were, me and my old high school friend, just catching up, smoking a joint, and who walks through the door? You guessed right: Random.

His face went pale when he saw me. He spent like 10 very awkward minutes there and left. He was part of that group, so we were doomed to see each other many times. I saw how small he was now, but I could also see for the first time that he was no tyrant, and that he felt even worse than me about what had happened. I had never seen that before. He almost stopped hanging out with those guys just because of my presence.

My high school friend who already knew my side of the story was driving around with him one day, and finally, after many years, he opened up. He told him that he barely remembered that night, and that he was extremely drunk and on drugs. However, he had the sense that he had done something really bad to me, and he felt so incredibly uncomfortable every time I was around.

United by a love of weed, we both kept hanging around the same people until eventually we became more relaxed around each other. I had already started to discover the magic of letting go, closing circles and healing from various therapies and books, so at a party I approached him and attacked the biggest elephant in the room. We talked, we said we were sorry, we forgave each other and moved on. I saw how he was as attached to that thing as much as I was, just on the opposite end of the rope. It´s easy to miss that when have the victim goggles on.

Releasing that pain and that hurt helped me to move forward, and to change the dynamics in my relationships.

It wasn't him I needed to forgive, but rather the action, the moment and the pain.

I was meant to be mad at the sin, not the sinner. It made it all easier.

Last year, Random and I were playing darts at a friend's house while everyone else was outside. There was not a slight lingering feeling or thought. He is a good guy and I am a good girl.

We are connected to those moments
or people that we cannot release.

They work in the shadows, coming up in the least expected moments and jumping at us like a crazed lion. It's not healthy, and it doesn't serve our current life and relationships.

Honestly, I have received so many blessings because of that precise encounter.

I realized at an early age that trying to fit in despite yourself is not the best route. I decided to study Psychology in order try and understand my reactions to that moment, which then led me to move to a different city and start a different life. I learned not to judge, or to listen and believe in any gossip. I developed more empathy for women. I worked harder, from the beginning, to remove any sexual stigmas or inhibitions, hence having a healthy, connected sexual life from an early age. That moment when I was 16 shaped me, and it's a big part of who I am now. I became more human.

So, do I have to thank him, or should I hate him? Honestly, I don't think I was in the wrong place at the wrong time. Somehow, I am sure it was meant to happen that way and that maybe, in our cosmic selves, we both agreed it would happen. I don't know if he also learned from this, or if it shaped him, as that is for him to know. I know he is a good guy and I also know some date rapists are good, but also very, very confused people.

The point is, you need to forgive and to find release within yourself for your own benefit, for you to move on and be free. You cannot whole-ass your life if you are dragging shit around like a hobo hoarder.

How many of these stories do you have? How much shit are you still dragging? You might not be as lucky as me, to have life constantly work to get you to see that behind the scenes, people are trying to do the best they can, but you have to grab the bull by the horns and face it. Ask for help, work on letting go of those stains on your heart and make it brand-new again.

I promise you that your real self has never been hurt, broken or dented. Your heart is always pristine, and it always shines pure love. Your only job is to get rid of any fences standing in the way of you and love. The good news is, if you built them, you can tear them down.

"Out beyond ideas of wrongdoing
and rightdoing there is a field.
I'll meet you there.
When the soul lies down
in that grass the world is
too full to talk about."

RUMI

KEEP IT REAL

To be whole-ass is to rip open your shirt, revealing your superhero attire underneath, abso-freaking-raw.

Ugh, the sound of the word "vulnerable" used to make me shrug like a raw oyster immersed in lemon juice. Disgusting! Who would want to be so transparent that everyone can see through you? Who would want to show themselves to the rest of the world? That's why masks were invented, right?

Wrong.

Vulnerability is a nuclear weapon to infuse love back into this planet. We just need to change our approach.

Sometimes we can feel that having our defenses down means we are open to attack or being hurt, but this doesn't have to be the case. You can be completely defenseless without it meaning that you are open to attacks, and you can be totally raw, exposed and still be rooted in the stillness that you are. You are human. You are meant to feel and live.

What would happen if little kids ran countries, the borders and the criminal courts? Yeah, maybe we would use chocolate and cookies as our currency, but we would get to see real people leading our territories and giving speeches. No more cardboard, rehearsed interactions, or strategies that come from greed and lust for power. No more rules just for the sake of making rules. How many people are in jail because of an accident? Why would we judge accidents? Kids know this.

It could be a mess, but at least it would be real.

The good news is that we were all kids, so we were all raw, and also that we as individuals create the collective. Waking up to vulnerability, one by one, can create communities of real people, real interactions and much more fun parties.

I think I've always been real, or at least I've always been real to what I believe is happening in the moment. Of course, sometimes, I look back and realize I was hiding something, or being a coward or whatever, but in the moment I always tend and try to be real.

It got me into lots of trouble, and sometimes it still does, but I am not afraid of pointing out the elephant in the room or showing and expressing exactly where I'm at in any moment. Yes, sometimes you know you are being irrational, or you know you are dropping a statement that will make people uncomfortable, but the only way to arrive at the other side is by crossing the river. Often, we attempt to teleport or to just appear on the other side without actually crossing the water, and most of the times this is futile.

We cannot skip moments. It's an impossibility.

The key to being real is being raw and vulnerable, and allowing yourself to be affected and impacted by life, by people and by events, even if it makes you cry. When did crying become so demonized, by the way? It's just freaking water coming out of our eyes! No one feels bad for peeing, unless of course they peed their pants in public.

Vulnerability makes us vibrate, as we feel life coursing through our veins. It makes the days seem less dull and much more exciting.

It takes so much energy to be stiff and cold, trying every day to not be affected by life, and not showing how life affects us. It´s so exhausting to behave in the "correct" way, always responding the way you think you should, and feeling something very unnatural about a certain situation. When you do this, you never allow things to come to the surface. Therefore, you probably don't learn from that situation, and are doomed to live it over and over again.

Don´t put your elbows on the table. Don´t eat with your legs crossed. Don´t say you don´t like something in front of your aunt. Don´t talk about certain topics with certain people. Always be polite. Don´t show you are upset at the dinner table. Pretend you are immune at work. Don´t let anyone see that Modern Family makes you cry.

Blah, blah, blah... boring, boring, boring... stiff, stiff humans.

No, señor.

I love my best friend – obviously, that´s why she is my best friend – but what I love most about her is that she is super real; the type of real that gets into trouble because she talks about taboo subjects, quite innocently, with stiff groups of people.

We can talk and be anything we are at any given moment. There is no hiding, no shoving feelings down the throat and no pretending to be something we are not. She dresses how she likes and laughs out loud. It's like a breath of fresh air to be with her, because I can be myself completely.

She never judges me when I am angry about a nonsensical thing, which then allows me to suddenly move on from that state and arrive at a more conscious discovery. She understands that I wouldn't have been able to arrive at a new place if it wasn't for feeling angry first.

You see what I mean? It's because she is real that she allows others to be real, and when people are being real, they can move on to a different state of being.

That is the magic of being real and embracing vulnerability.

Being real allows others to be real,
to start discovering their true selves,
maybe for the first time.

"What happens when
people open their hearts?"

"They get better."

Haruki Murakami. Norwegian Wood (1987)

TAKE CHANCES OVER AND OVER

Vulnerability goes hand in hand with openness.

Let's put it this way: vulnerability is the willingness to feel, to be impacted, to experience life and to be transparent. Openness means dissolving the lining that appears to be within us and the rest of the world, and giving the universe an open pathway to deliver to us whatever it is we are meant to live in this world.

Everyone's life is meant to be an adventure.

I don't mean that you should be flying airplanes solo, or climbing mountains before having evening cocktails with Elton John. You might have the simplest of lives, yet still be on a wonderful adventure full of every day blessings.

The problems start when we are not open.

Maybe we learned that life is difficult, or that we are sinners, or that do not deserve a blessed life. Maybe, one time, you had a dream, but your surroundings shut it off by telling you that life is a series of A+B+C in a linear path, and therefore dreams don't come true. The whole idea of sacrifice is well ingrained in Christian culture.

But what if it wasn't quite like that? What if we are in fact divine children, born on this Earth to experience a shower of divine gifts, with full support to live our wildest dreams? If you absolutely knew that this was your nature, how then would you live your life?

Waking up every day and knowing that the whole universe is singing your praises, and is here to serve you, gives a completely different meaning to your life. Being wide open to receiving, to being surprised or to being carried and supported takes a lot of the pressure off.

It's one thing to be whole-ass while fighting the world, but being whole-ass while knowing you have all the help you will ever need is something else altogether.

A long time ago, I was on a train to Paris. My Canadian friends were on their way there, and I had just had a terrible experience in Marseille. I hopped on the train, and when I went to grab something to eat, I met a man and his son. He was a bit older than me, and I didn't get a vibe that he has hitting on me. He was very polite.

During the course of our conversation, I told him that I was going to Paris for a vacation. It was my first time in Paris. We didn't know how long we were staying, and we didn't know where we were staying, as we had only booked a hotel for one night. Then he said: *"Well, I am leaving tomorrow for a two-week trip, so you and your friends can stay at my apartment if you like."*

My first reaction was to say no, as tons of thoughts and judgments jumped around my head. Then he added: *"My girlfriend will be there for a few days, and then she is off, too. If you guys don't mind sharing with her."* I thanked him for the offer and we exchanged numbers. I was willing to ditch the offer, but he texted me afterward with his address, and I decided to be open.

The next day, we showed up at his apartment. It was a beautiful flat close to Montmartre, with a view of the Eiffel Tower. We were ecstatic. We had the best of times. His girlfriend was a sweetheart who took us for dinner and dancing, and we were able to stay for longer thanks to saving money on hotel costs.

It wasn't the last time I stayed in that apartment, as by chance, when I went to Paris again he was away again.

I could've said no. I could've thought there was something dodgy or weird about it, but I didn't, and it turned out fantastically well.

So many stories like that, so many blessings that are constantly trying to come our way, but sometimes we resemble a ninja, rejecting everything with a suspicious look on our face.

It doesn't mean you should be naïve, and it doesn't mean you should respond to those email chains that supposedly come from the prince of a faraway land, asking you for money. It simply means that you should be open, as if someone told you that they have a surprise for you, but you have to be attentive all day to discover it.

The question is:

***Are you willing to live the maximum
reality that is available to you?***

Or would you settle for just the bare minimum? Living the greatest reality available requires courage, a willingness to step out of your comfort zone and a trust that every step will be revealed not one second before it's necessary.

The rewards are gigantic. Being fearless and bold fills you up with life force and with love for what you do, both in life and for everyone around you.

And that´s what being open entails. You can only fill water up to the top of the pitcher, so be a huge-ass pitcher, as wide open as you can possibly be.

Always be willing to let go of any resistance you encounter, and of every little hint of a "No" that you perceive. Notice how most of our closedness comes from assumptions and conclusions we made a long time ago, which now we know are completely senseless.

Remember, every attribute is a habit. You can build up a new way of being just by making the conscious effort to do so. By exploring and being super alert, you can change at any time, until you become a whole-ass version of yourself.

And it can start with the silliest things.

I used to be really self-conscious. I´ve always been weird and silly, but only with my super-close friends. Appearing silly in front of others would make me feel so uncomfortable and strange.

When I moved to Barcelona to study acting, I met two of the greatest friends I could ever ask for. He, Borja, is Spanish, and she, Adelaida, is Colombian. The three of us met at school and immediately clicked, and for the next three years we were inseparable.

Given the nature of actors, they were shameless. They taught me how to act stupid in front of people. Think about it – it's just a passing moment. Most of the people you are surrounded by do not have a face, and you will never see them again. I saw how limited I could be, and how I could stop the fun just because I cared about the rest.

So, I learned to look ugly in pictures, to dance weirdly at a bar and to pretend to be someone else in a subway. And what happened? That attitude starting leaking into other areas. I became more willing to sing in public, the creativity I used in my characters was applied more freely in real life, and I could write and invent songs in a much more fluid way.

All because those two taught me to be silly and to not care.

That's how it starts. Openness begins wherever you want it to, just as long you want it to.

"Imagine you have been standing in a golden river of grace for all your life, and you have been ignorant to it."

Maharishi Krishnananda Ishaya

GRACE AND HER RIVER

Imagine you are invited to a movie premiere. It's one of those fancy Hollywood premieres, where everyone gets all dressed up and walks the red carpet before entering the theater.

First, you receive a package with the most beautiful dress, or suit, you have ever seen. Later on, you receive a box filled with the most luxurious presents, and it's all part of the movie premiere experience. Then, you are wondering how you are going to do your makeup and hair, and teams of professionals walk through your door and make you look like Grace Kelly.

You call an Uber to get to the theater, and when you walk outside, an incredibly classy Mercedes limousine is there to pick you up, and your best friends are inside... all part of the movie experience!

There is a never-ending shower of presents from the moment you arrive at the theater, starting with you walking the red carpet with Chris Hemsworth. All the way through the movie, you feel loved, pampered and extremely taken care of by the whole production staff, and let's not even get started on the after party.

Being rooted in the present moment is like constantly attending a movie premiere. You are the guest -the watcher- and the whole production of life, titled *The Universe*, is constantly showering you with presents. This is not something available only to some saints and sages. It is there for every single human being on Earth.

The thing is, most of us spend the majority of our lives in some other moment, and seldom do we appear right here, right now, in the only moment that actually breathes and lives, where grace exists.

The river of grace never dries out, but we become so busy holding on with all we've got, holding onto the past moments, that we completely miss out on it.

> *Deep down there is a belief that we don't deserve all available grace, so we allow just a tiny bit.*

It's as if you were a kid at your own birthday party, and when you open the first present you hold on to it with all your strength, because you believe it is the only present coming to you. All the kids are handing over their presents to you, and your parents keep telling to put the present down so that you can see the rest, but you are scared that if you let go of that one single present, nothing else will come your way.

You are so focused on that present, focusing on your feelings of being undeserving, that you will not, in any way, simply let go. All the other presents go to waste, and you are left wondering why your friends don't love you more, and why you only got one present.

That is exactly how it works. The whole universe is constantly trying to shower us with never-ending presents, but we hold on so tightly to what we already have that we miss out on anything new that could come our way.

Why?

Because you believe that the life you live is yours. You believe that your thoughts are yours, your feelings are yours and your experiences of relationships are yours. And you try to keep them all, holding them so that you feel bigger because of the number of things you possess.

What if life wasn't yours? What if your only job here was to constantly watch a movie premiere while you are showered and pampered?

It's a strange concept to comprehend on an intellectual level, but the experience of it, even for one moment, is worth a thousand words. Nothing belongs to you, and trust me, once you experience that, you won't want it any other way.

Letting go is the art that enables grace to flow.

The more you let go, the more it comes. Earth and human life is not torture; it's not a sick, twisted game that the angels play, as they have fun watching us being closed down in pain and suffering, wondering how the Hell we can endure.

This place is meant to be Heaven on Earth. You simply need to let go. Let go of all you think you know, let go of all the thoughts and feelings and let them be, since they are only passing by. Let go of all your attachments to how things should look. Let go of your tendency to be distracted from this divine present moment. Let go of your small, tiny self and of your identity. You are way more infinite than that.

You are the infinite itself, and grace is your natural state.

In Closing

WHOLE-ASS WORLD
Remember Who You Are

You are magic. You are existence itself bottled up in a human body. Your real self exists beyond the confines of this galaxy.

There is nothing small about you, and you are here, right at this moment in time, for a reason. You came to complete an important mission, and all of your experiences have been designed to show you what that mission is. There is no such thing as a mediocre life in the Big Plan. No one is here to just tag along.

It's my dream that no human on Earth arrives at the end of their life feeling repentant for not having lived to their maximum potential.

Be wild, be open, be willing to change, dare to love, be simple, be wise, follow your dreams with passion, infuse your every day with purpose, soar through the limitations of your mind and see for yourself that the being that exists beneath is the most wonderful of beings: you.

You have the power to change this world, starting with yourself. You are the agent that this world needs right now. Do not wait for someone else to step up.

Be willing to shed skins as many times as necessary. Transform into the person that you want to be. You can start right now, no process necessary. Big and real changes start with one moment, one decision, one choice. You have that ability in you, so use it.

And for the sake of all humanity, do it now. We need you to start living your life's purpose. Everyone needs to be in their place and play their part for this Earth to become the heaven that it was always intended for it to be.

Imagine a world where only happy humans exist. Imagine a world where love, fraternity, abundance and beauty are the pillars of society. Imagine what it would look like – how the houses, the roads, science, activities, interactions, transportation and families would look and behave. It is not only possible to have this world; it's also our right. It doesn't need to take much time.

And it starts with you.

There is no time to lose. Why would you want to waste time? Why would you want to live a life half-assed? Would you really be content with that?

Are you really happy, feeling like your days are full of life and love? Do you really go to bed with a smile on your face? Do you really wake up every morning with a desire to see what the day presents? Do you really connect with other humans and serve, laugh and enjoy? Are you putting your talents to use in the service of humanity?

If so, great. Thank you for participating in the world and being an agent of change. If not, join us, as we need you now. Use these tools, discover your own tools and start weaving the new reality.

It´s imminent. We all have to wake up and remember what we are here for. Now!

When I was a child, I read an article in *Reader´s Digest* about the future. It painted a picture of everything so automated that humans would have all the time in the world to enjoy life, to travel, to be creative and to explore. However, we have instead set-up a strange world where we have to work to survive, and we survive only to perish, but that is not the only possible outcome. We can alter this outcome and be free.

Everything in this world has changed, and it will continue to change forevermore. Nothing is stagnant. Look around and see how the world looks nothing like it did 50 years ago, and certainly nothing like it did 400 years ago. The idea that the world will stay the same is a result of us only seeing the small picture. We are only one fragment of the tapestry of humanity. This decade is nothing but a blink of an eye. This world is nothing but the product of the humans who inhabit it at any given time. We are not dependent on, or victims of, the future; the future depends on us. World leaders are nothing without the collective.

It´s time to stop believing that we have no choice over the fate of the Earth. We do.

All major changes across the history of humanity happened because of a human being. Every huge discovery, every social revolution, every change in the paradigm of the collective started with just a few, and those few started with one. It only takes one open vessel to allow something new to be downloaded onto this Earth.

Everything can change in the blink of an eye.

The question is, are you in or are you out? Are you going to keep being dragged, or are you willing to step up and wake up, so that the divine can come through you?

Now is the time.

Let the wildest game begin.

About the Author

Maharani – Cristina García Reyes – is an Ishaya monk who teaches The Bright Path Ascension courses around the world. As a monk she has meditated extensively and committed her life to increasing consciousness in the world by increasing it in herself.

She grew up in a town in Mexico called Chihuahua -yes, like the dog and no, they are not related. She took off at age nineteen and has since lived in Mexico and Canada and currently resides with her partner in a tiny mountain-top village in Spain, near to the main retreat center of the Ishayas.

Maharani has been a writer since age 6, when she won her school's poetry contest with a poem called "Love". Fascinated by the human condition and consciousness, she is known for writing with an inspiring realness and highly relatable vulnerability. You can follow here blog online over at her website. She also does one-to-one sessions to guide and support people in switching their perspective, gaining clarity and being uncompromisingly whole-assed.

Reference List:

Dr. Strange. (2016). [film] Scott. Derrickson. dir. USA: Marvel Studios.

Ishaya, N. (2012). Chit Happens. Carlsbad: Balboa Press.

Murakami, H. (1987). Norwegian Wood. Tokio: Kodansha.

Palahniuk, C. (1996). Fight Club. New York: W.W. Norton.

Parks and Recreation, Episode 62, Sweet Sixteen. 2012. NBC. February, 23.

Reality Bites. (1994). [film] Ben Stiller. dir. USA: Jersey Films.

Shlain, T. And Let it Ripple Film Studio (2014). The Science of Character. [video] Available at: https://www.youtube.com/watch?v=U3nT2KDAGOc

Straus, J. (2006). Unhooked Generation. 1st ed. [ebook] New York: Hyperion. Available at: https://www.amazon.com/Unhooked-Generation-Truth-About-Single/dp/B003A02YZG

Walker, B. (2009). Hua Hu Ching: The Unknown Teachings of Lao Tzu. San Fransisco: HarperOne.

We bought a zoo. (2011). [film] Cameron Crowe. dir. USA: Vinyl Films, LBI Entertainment, Dune Entertainment.